Specific Learning Difficulties

(Dyslexia)

A Teachers' Guide

"While the special needs of some children will continue for relatively long periods and, in some cases, permanently, those of other children will, if promptly and effectively met, cease to exist."
Mary Warnock.

Produced by:

Margaret Crombie B.A.(Hons), Dip.C.E., A.M.B.D.A., Dip.Cur.Dev.(Sp.L.D.), Dip.S.E.N.

Further details of other publications can be found in the free catalogue which is available from:

Sales and Publications,
University of Strathclyde,
Faculty of Education, Jordanhill Campus,
76 Southbrae Drive, Glasgow G13 1PP.

Telephone: 0141 950 3170   Fax: 0141 950 3171

October 1994
© University of Strathclyde
ISBN 1 85098 485 9   B.474

INTRODUCTION

At a conservative estimate one in twenty-five people is dyslexic. This means that in most classes there is at least one puzzling child who seems erratic in his learning, and who is struggling with the reading and spelling skills which the teacher expects of him. This makes survival in the classroom very difficult for that child. But we know from experience that there are children who do survive, and go on to fulfil their potential in learning. These are usually the children who at some point have met with a teacher who was sympathetic and informed about dyslexic difficulties.

When faced with a worried parent, asking, "Do you think my child may be dyslexic?", the teacher has often had to fall back on rather defensive and evasive answers. Up till now it has been hard to find clear, comprehensive advice for a school to follow. This Guide fills that information gap, providing coherent and accessible information for the classroom teacher.

The Guide answers the teachers' questions about the nature and incidence of dyslexia. It gives a checklist of possible "symptoms" for both primary and secondary school students, and illustrates the points with two useful profiles of children. It provides practical ideas for classroom support, and also explains where to turn for help, when sympathy and general support are not enough.

In this well-researched document, the appendices contain a wealth of information and references, and will be well thumbed by anyone in schools interested in helping children with literacy difficulties.

Margaret Crombie is an experienced classroom teacher and learning support teacher with a special interest and qualifications in dyslexia/SpLD. The Guide is an excellent distillation of her experience, and as such will be welcomed by class and specialist teachers as well as other professionals. This practical and useful reference book should be available in every school.

Jean Walker

Acknowledgements

Grateful thanks to Jean Walker, Dyslexia Institute Principal of Training
(N.E. England and Scotland), for writing the Introduction and for her advice and
helpful comments during the compilation of this Guide.

Also to Reading Centre colleagues for sharing the benefits of their experience.

And to my husband, Alan, for patient help on the technical aspects of editing and
presentation of the material.

Contents

TERMINOLOGY 1

HOW TO USE THE GUIDE 2

THE NATURE OF SPECIFIC LEARNING DIFFICULTIES 3

HOW COMMON IS THE PROBLEM? 4

HOW CAN WE RECOGNISE THE DYSLEXIC CHILD? 5

INITIAL OBSERVATIONS WHICH MAY POINT TO SpLD. 6
EARLY PRIMARY 6
   In language work 6
   In other areas 7
LATER STAGES 8

THE ROUTE TO ASSESSMENT 9

RECORDING A CHILD'S NEEDS (STATEMENTING). 10

ASSESSMENT 11
WHAT TO LOOK FOR IN THE RESULTS 13

WHAT CAN THE CLASS TEACHER DO TO ALLEVIATE PROBLEMS? 18

WHAT ARE STRUCTURED CUMULATIVE MULTISENSORY METHODS? 20

MEETING THE CHILD'S SPECIFIC NEEDS IN VARIOUS AREAS OF THE CURRICULUM 21

SPECIFIC HELP IN VARIOUS AREAS OF THE CURRICULUM 22
LANGUAGE WORK 22
   Reading 22
   Spelling 28
   Handwriting 31
   Continuous Prose Writing 34
MATHEMATICS 37
PHYSICAL EDUCATION 43
TOPIC WORK 44
THE CREATIVE ARTS 44

IMPROVING CURRICULUM-SUPPORTIVE SKILLS 45
MEMORY 45
MOTIVATION 47

CURRICULAR SUPPORT AT THE SECONDARY STAGE 48

EPILOGUE 50

APPENDICES 51
APPENDIX 1 ASSESSMENT MATERIAL 51
   LANGUAGE 51
   MATHEMATICS 52
   INTELLIGENCE 53
   USEFUL BOOKS FOR THE TEACHER 53
APPENDIX 2 LANGUAGE MATERIALS 54
   Reading 54
     For Topic Work 55

Spelling 55
Handwriting 56
Written Language Work 56
Spelling Dictionaries 57
Computer Software 57
Useful Books for Teachers 59
APPENDIX 3 GAMES 61
APPENDIX 4 USEFUL ADDRESSES 62
APPENDIX 5 COURSES IN SpLD FOR TEACHERS 65
APPENDIX 6 BIBLIOGRAPHY 66

Index 69

TERMINOLOGY

While "specific learning difficulties" (SpLD) is the preferred term for use amongst professionals involved in the education field, non-professionals, parents and many of the children themselves may prefer to use the term "dyslexia". Either term is acceptable and teachers should be prepared to use whatever term is most relevant to the situation and to those with whom they are communicating. Priority should be given to assessing and alleviating the child's difficulties, not to debating the labels we attach to them.

As there is a lack of a suitable adjective to match the term "specific learning difficulties", rather than constantly repeat "the person/child with specific learning difficulties", I have chosen to use the more concise term "dyslexic".

The word "child" does not convey any information as to sex. Because there is no similarly neutral personal pronoun in English, I have used the pronoun "he" to refer to the dyslexic child, there being more dyslexic boys than girls. The ratio is estimated to be around 4:1. The principles and methods dealt with, however, apply equally to both sexes.

HOW TO USE THE GUIDE

In producing this guide, the intention is to provide ideas for teachers on how they can best help dyslexic children in the classroom situation. Indications are given to enable the classroom teacher to identify possible cases of specific learning difficulties and direction is given on how, where and when to obtain appropriate advice and assistance. Most of the suggestions offered are not new. Rather this is an attempt to amalgamate some of the existing good practice into an easy-to-follow guide, and where possible extend some of the ideas or recommend appropriate source material.

Guidelines are given on assessment and on the various areas of the curriculum which may be affected by the child's difficulties. Suggestions are made at various points indicating material which may help the dyslexic child. The Appendices contain details of such materials and where they may be obtained. No attempt has been made to produce a complete list of such resources as the amount of material is vast, new resource material is constantly coming on to the market and previous material goes out of print or becomes outdated. Suggestions therefore are only a guide to the types of material available. Children will inevitably differ in the degree to which they are affected by their specific learning difficulties and the methods used will require to be adapted to individual needs.

Local authority provision for children with specific learning difficulties will vary from area to area and each authority will have its own procedure for helping dyslexic children. Teachers will require to establish the level of support which is available to them from outside agencies and what must be provided by their own school staff.

Within the United Kingdom, there are differences too in the actual legalities and terms used. For example, where we in Scotland will refer to a **Record of Needs** for a child who is experiencing severe difficulties, in England and Wales, the child would require to have a **Statement**. (These terms will be explained more fully later.) We as teachers must be aware of these differences and how they are likely to affect the children we work with.

THE NATURE OF SPECIFIC LEARNING DIFFICULTIES

It is very difficult to find one single definition which will accurately describe the exact nature of the difficulties experienced as these vary considerably among those involved. Children may experience learning difficulties for a variety of reasons and this is evident in their learning as seen in the classroom situation. Some pupils are generally slow to learn and develop skills at a slower pace, never quite reaching the level of their peers. These children could be said to have **general** learning difficulties.

For other children however, the difficulties only apply in certain areas of their work, particularly where processing symbolic information is concerned. Teachers and parents are often puzzled by these children particularly when there is a very marked and apparent difference between their educational attainments and their overall ability level. These are the children to whom we would apply the term **specific** learning difficulties. These **specific** difficulties are likely to affect areas such as perception, working memory, discrimination, motor coordination, sequencing and orientation, and manifest themselves in difficulty in learning to read, spell and produce written language work. They may also overlap into other areas of the curriculum, such as mathematics and physical education. Behaviour too may well be affected.

It must be noted however that there is a very wide spectrum of specific learning difficulties, and that these difficulties vary considerably between those affected mildly and the very severe cases. Individual children are also likely to exhibit a different pattern of difficulties. Assessment to diagnose specific learning difficulties must therefore investigate all the areas likely to be affected and consider how these match the child's potential ability level. We can then use the areas of strength to develop the weak areas.

HOW COMMON IS THE PROBLEM?

Specific learning difficulties, like many other conditions, varies greatly in degree of severity. On the one hand, we have the child who has initial confusions over letters, sounds and sequencing, but who gets over his problems by the time he is seven or eight, and only occasionally faces a real difficulty, often over spelling, at later stages. On the other hand, we can have a child who fails to learn to read completely despite the efforts of successive teachers, who is totally unable to tackle written work beyond the point of writing his name, and even that may contain a sequencing error or reversal. In between, we inevitably have the whole range of severity of difficulties. If however, we consider a child who is reading around two years or more behind his chronological age, and who is experiencing sufficient difficulty with his written language work that it is extremely difficult, if not impossible, for the teacher to comprehend what is meant, then the proportion of children with specific learning difficulties is around 3.5%. This will mean that in the average school, there are at least a handful of such children.

HOW CAN WE RECOGNISE THE DYSLEXIC CHILD?

It is the responsibility of every classroom teacher to recognise the signs of specific learning difficulties and to carry out, or arrange for, preliminary assessment. This should be performed in cooperation with the school's learning support co-ordinator and the headteacher. Parents also need to be made aware of the problems the child is encountering. In areas which have peripatotic learning support specialists, then valuable help should be available from this source. When specific learning difficulties are suspected, help in devising a suitable programme can then be arranged.

If, after a few months on this programme, there is still no significant progress, a more definitive assessment can be arranged. An educational psychologist should establish the severity of the problem and what additional help the child requires. The possibility of the child acquiring a **Record of Needs** or **Statement** may also require to be considered in the light of the psychologist's findings. Possible channels to go through for help in organising a suitable programme and arranging further assessment are set out in the flow chart on page 9. These will however vary slightly between different areas.

The checklist on the following pages provides a rough guide as to likely areas which may be affected. Many of the points are common during a child's first year at school. If, however, several of the indicators persist very much beyond this stage, more detailed assessment is necessary. Specific learning difficulties may exist across the whole spectrum of intellectual ability. It is often the marked **discrepancy** between the child's **intellectual ability** as exhibited in his verbal performance, or his very good spatial ability, and his **reading and written language skills,** which leads the teacher to suspect specific difficulties.

INITIAL OBSERVATIONS WHICH MAY POINT TO Sp.L.D.

EARLY PRIMARY

In language work

(1) Poor reading progress on look-and-say or phonic methods.

(2) Severe difficulty with spelling. Sometimes apparently bizarre spellings.

(3) Considerable confusion over simple punctuation and grammar.

(4) Confusion of letters similar in shape: b/d/p/q; u/n; f/t; M/W.

(5) Omission or confusion of small words: the, a, so, to, of, from, for.

(6) Badly or wrongly formed letters.

(7) Uncertainty about when and where to use lower and upper case letters.

(8) Reversals of letters and whole words: "was" for "saw"; "god" for "dog".

(9) Confusion of similar sounding letters: d/t; v/f/th; short vowels.

(10) Faulty auditory sequencing in reading and in the repetition of words: "permilinary" for "preliminary"; "emeny" for "enemy", "pasghetti" for "spaghetti".

(11) Foreshortening of words in written work: "permance" for "performance", "intring" for "interesting".

(12) Difficulty in finding a name for an object.

(13) Transposals: sift for fist.

(14) Fusion of the letters in words: *our* for *out*.

(15) Difficulty in remembering what day it is, his birthday, his address or telephone number.

(16) Possible history of slow speech development.

(17) Difficulty in copying from the blackboard.

(18) Difficulty or extreme tenseness in holding pencil.

In other areas

(19) Difficulty in sequencing: days of the week, months of the year, the alphabet, word order in a sentence, number bonds, multiplication tables.

(20) Confusion over directionality: left/right, up/down, to/past on clock or watch.

(21) Difficulty in remembering a short sequence: numbers, instructions etc.

(22) Mixed laterality.

(23) Family history of reading and spelling problems.

(24) Difficulty in understanding concepts such as yesterday/today/tomorrow.

(25) Problems with simple mental arithmetic.

Often the class teacher senses intuitively that this is a "puzzling, underachieving child". The importance of this should not be overlooked. It is suggested that in cases where a group of these indicators (more than six) persist into the child's second year of schooling, the classroom teacher should note the precise difficulties early in the first term. If specific learning difficulties are severe, they may be apparent even earlier than this. In which case, steps should be taken during the child's first year at school.

The class teacher should draw in any skilled help which is available both within the school and in the local area. As mentioned, this will, of course, require the involvement of the headteacher. Advice and materials and sometimes cooperative teaching support may then be available. Records should be kept of the nature of the help given and the results observed. If, six months later, there is little or no improvement in spite of the cooperative efforts to remedy the situation, then further more precise assessment by the teacher will be necessary to establish more accurately the level of the child's ability and precise areas of difficulty. At this point, some form of norm-referenced testing is appropriate - not for the purpose of comparing the child with his peers, but to establish if the child is falling **significantly** below the level which we should expect for his age. Rather than highlight an individual child and to avoid any unnecessary embarrassment, many of the items can be observed in group activities, profiles being kept relating to particular children.

LATER STAGES

For the child suspected of having specific learning difficulties who is only discovered at a later stage (Upper Primary or Secondary), the following checklist will be more appropriate. Again a group of indicators would suggest the need for further investigation.

(1) Intellectual capacity and comprehension level significantly greater than performance in reading or written work.

(2) Failing completely at reading, or reading just adequately in the early stages, with ability insufficient to cope in upper primary and early secondary stages.

(3) Mechanics of reading weak, inserting or omitting words, guessing, ignoring phrasing and punctuation marks.

(4) Avoidance of reading whenever possible, never reading for pleasure.

(5) Failure to spell adequately to allow the reader to understand.

(6) Inconsistency in spelling, even of previously memorised words.

(7) Omission of letters or whole syllables, or addition of inappropriate ones.

(8) Poor use of syntax.

(9) Mispronunciation, misuse or inability to retain words for verbal use.

(10) Misunderstanding due to inadequacy of reading ability - e.g. reading "hysterical" for "historical".

(11) Difficulty in understanding sequences read aloud or in comprehending directions.

(12) Difficulty in answering questions which rely on the interpretation of own written work.

(13) Difficulty remembering the sequential movement patterns necessary for letter formation, resulting in poorly formed and disordered presentation.

(14) Inability to remember words and phrases which are dictated.

Initially, the class teacher must ensure that the child has his eyesight tested and that an audiometric test of hearing has been carried out recently. This can be checked from the child's medical records and if problems are suspected, may require the involvement of the school medical practitioner with possibility of further referral to orthoptist or audiometrician.

A number of children with SpLD have been found to have poor vergence control of the eyes. For children under the age of eight and a half, monocular occlusion (wearing a pair of spectacles with one lens occluded) for reading may be of help. For older children, vergence exercises are often more beneficial. These require the child to be referred to a skilled orthoptist and recommendations can only be made after a complete assessment of eye vergence has been completed. An orthoptist is available at most main hospitals. Parents must of course be kept informed at all stages, referral being made through either the school medical officer or the child's general practitioner. It must be stressed that this is not a cure for SpLD, but will ensure that existing difficulties are not being aggravated unnecessarily.

THE ROUTE TO ASSESSMENT

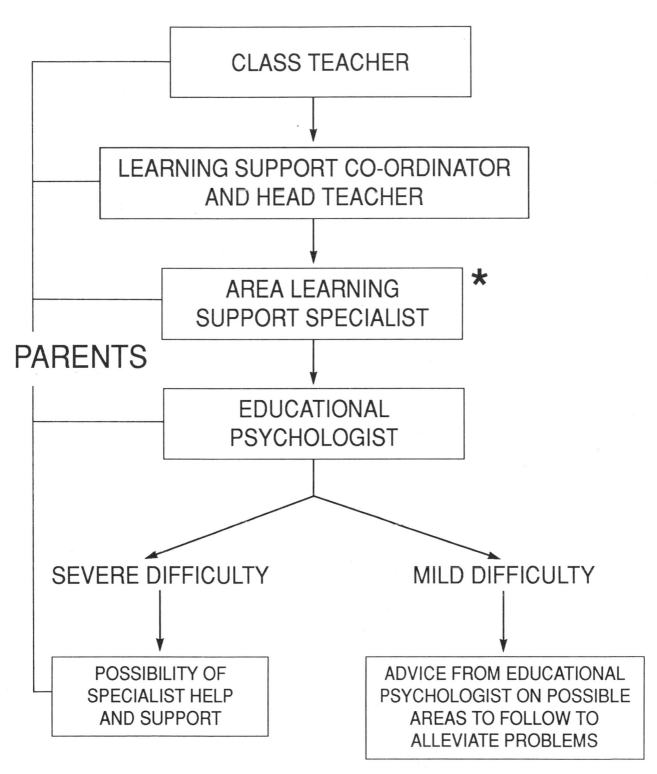

* This may not be available in all areas.

RECORDING A CHILD'S NEEDS (STATEMENTING).

There are a number of important differences between the law in Scotland and that in England and Wales. One important difference is in the terms used. According to The Education (Scotland) Act, 1981, a child will require to have a **Record of Needs** if he has "pronounced, specific or complex special educational needs which are such as require continuing review". In England and Wales, the similar act states that a child should be the subject of a **Statement** if he has "special educational needs which call for the authority to determine the special educational provision that should be made".

The specified contents of Records vary slightly from those of Statements, but both must contain details of the authority's assessment of special educational needs and the provision which should be made to meet these needs. The authority has an obligation to meet special educational needs and the Record or Statement acts as a contract between the authority and parents/ guardians. Children who have mild SpLD are unlikely to require a Record of Needs or Statement, as their difficulties can generally be met within the ordinary classroom curriculum without the necessity for special arrangements. However children with severe SpLD who cannot access the curriculum without significant extra help are likely to require one.

With the increasing demands being put upon both children and teachers by the introduction of testing from the age of seven, it has become more important than ever that children who have difficulties are not made to feel a failure because they cannot reach the attainment targets achieved by their peers. Therefore any provision which will help give children access to the 5-14 programme (Scotland) or National Curriculum (England & Wales) should be considered a priority. While allowances should be available for important exams without a Statement or Record, it might make obtaining suitable provision considerably easier. In cases where you feel a child might benefit, the possibility of opening a Record or Statement should be discussed with your school's educational psychologist.

ASSESSMENT

Examples of appropriate material for assessment of children displaying a group of indicators would be:

1. Aston Index (L.D.A.) gives a profile for the child of Primary School age who is displaying difficulties, and contains tests of vocabulary, word recognition, spelling, visual and auditory sequential memory, sound discrimination, free writing etc. The handbook contained in the kit gives full details of how to interpret the results. As many of the tests require to be conducted individually, the administration of the whole Index is very time-consuming. If skilled assistance can be brought in from outwith the classroom to help, this will relieve demands on the class teacher's time.

2. "The Macmillan Diagnostic Reading Pack" by Ted Ames (NFER-Nelson) covers diagnosis at four stages in the development of reading skills - corresponds approximately to reading ages of 5+, 6+, 7+ and 8+.

3. Either
   a. "New Macmillan Reading Analysis" (NFER-Nelson)
                          or
   b. "Neale Analysis of Reading Ability - Revised British Edition" (NFER-Nelson) gives qualitative assessment of individual reading difficulties, and supplementary diagnostic material to highlight specific areas of difficulty.

      Either the Macmillan Analysis or the Neale can be used to assess reading attainment as well as to diagnose types of difficulty, through presenting passages of increasing difficulty.

      Age range for Macmillan Reading Analysis is from seven to over eleven. It can also be used with older pupils who have reading difficulties. For Neale, age range is from seven to thirteen, and is therefore useful for both Primary and Secondary school age children with reading problems. Both give indications of comprehension skills.

4. Vernon's "Graded Word Spelling Test", (Hodder and Stoughton) gives a Spelling Age score from 6 to 16+ years.

5. Clay's "Early Detection of Reading Difficulties: A Diagnostic Survey" (Heinemann) provides a screening device with a non-normative approach. It is designed for diagnosing reading difficulties in children who are not making good progress after their first year's reading instruction.

6. Professor Miles' "Bangor Dyslexia Test" (L.D.A.) is a screening device to determine whether difficulties are typically dyslexic or not. The test can be used from the age of seven, but caution has to be used with children as young as this, as dyslexic-type difficulties (such as b/d confusion) may persist till around the age of eight in a child who is not dyslexic.

7. "English Picture Vocabulary" Tests 1, 2 and 3. (Education Evaluation Enterprises) were designed to assess levels of listening vocabulary, and are independent of spoken language or reading ability on the part of the testee. Test 1 is for administration to individual children. Test 2 is suitable for both individuals or groups and Test 3 is available only in the group form. Age range covered by the first two is 5 to 11 and for Test 3, range is 11 to 18 years.

8. A sample of the child's free writing should be evaluated.

A broad sample of suitable material has been quoted. This is in the hope that every school will have at least sufficient of these tests available to give a profile of the child's weaknesses and strengths. If not available within the school, then it would be hoped that a local Teachers' Centre would be able to help.

See Appendix 1 for further details of materials and the age groups for which they are suited, names of publishers etc. The suggestions include both norm and criterion-referenced materials. The norm-referenced products will be useful in determining our pupil profile and will help us establish just how far behind our pupil has fallen. The criterion-referenced materials will help us know exactly what we should plan to teach and will be useful in drawing up a teaching programme.

WHAT TO LOOK FOR IN THE RESULTS

For a complete assessment the teacher needs to be satisfied that the child's whole profile is being considered and that there is a complete picture of strengths and weaknesses. The Aston Index kit together with an assessment of intellectual ability should provide an initial indication of whether or not the child has specific learning difficulties. The following pages set out the types of profiles we might look for. Assessment, while it may be carried out by the classroom teacher, may require additional help from specialists outwith. If there is doubt, it is best to seek specialist advice.

For the teacher to suspect specific learning difficulties, we would expect both Reading and Spelling to be considerably below what we would anticipate for the child's level of intellectual ability. The test used to calculate Mental Age, which forms part of the Aston Index, is however not a reliable one. As a test of intellectual ability, it cannot be used to rule out any children. If there is suspicion of specific learning difficulties from the other parts of the assessment, and the child fails to respond to immediate intervention to improve matters, then the psychologist's assessment will give a much more satisfactory and reliable indication of the child's potential.

If we consider a child with an IQ of around 100, we would expect his Reading and Spelling Ages to be *roughly* in line with his Chronological Age. A child with an IQ of 120-130, then would be expected to have a Reading Age considerably in advance of his Chronological Age, and the reverse also applies. For a child with an IQ of 80, we would not be surprised to find Reading and Spelling Ages were behind Chronological Age. A Mental Age can be calculated by multiplying the child's Chronological Age by his IQ, and dividing the result by 100.

We must always bear in mind the limitations of IQ tests and therefore of assessing a Mental Age score. The figures arrived at do not remain fixed throughout life. There is also the possibility that they were obtained on an *off day*. The scores are nonetheless useful provided they are used in a positive way for the sole purpose of comparing a child's attainment with his likely capabilities.

For example,

JOHN   AGE 9 YEARS

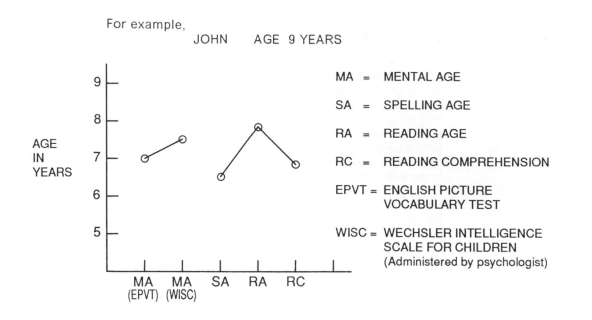

MA = MENTAL AGE

SA = SPELLING AGE

RA = READING AGE

RC = READING COMPREHENSION

EPVT = ENGLISH PICTURE VOCABULARY TEST

WISC = WECHSLER INTELLIGENCE SCALE FOR CHILDREN
(Administered by psychologist)

PERFORMANCE ON TEST MATERIAL

John, age 9 could be categorised in the moderate *general* learning difficulties category. He has a Mental Age calculated to be at the seven to seven-and-a-half year level. His Spelling Age at six-and-a-half years is below this. His Reading Accuracy is just as we would anticipate and comprehension at 6.9 years is not unexpected. A sample of free writing is shown below.

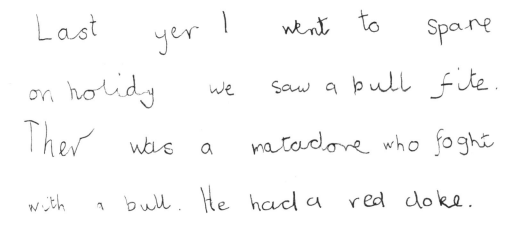

From his errors, we can see that John has absorbed much of the information he has been taught. He has some difficulties in remembering the actual spellings of words, but has gained benefit from training in phonic skills. He is approaching the spelling of words in a sensible fashion. Handwriting, while still immature shows that most letters are correctly formed and there are no apparent problems with directionality. John comes from a stable home background. Both parents live at home. While they have no particular training, the parents are anxious to help John at home and will cooperate as much as possible to ensure that John achieves his potential.

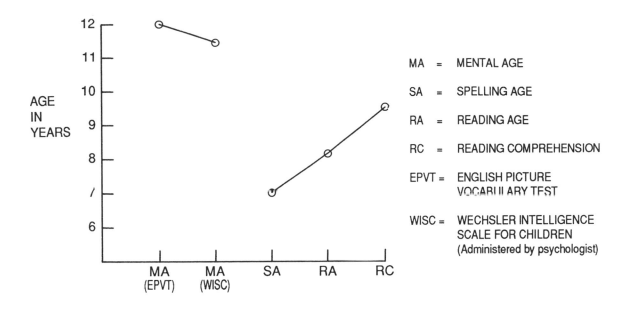

WENDY   AGE 10.2 YEARS

MA = MENTAL AGE

SA = SPELLING AGE

RA = READING AGE

RC = READING COMPREHENSION

EPVT = ENGLISH PICTURE
VOCABULARY TEST

WISC = WECHSLER INTELLIGENCE
SCALE FOR CHILDREN
(Administered by psychologist)

UNDERLYING ABILITY AND ATTAINMENT

Wendy, aged ten years and two months has a Mental Age calculated to be between eleven-and-a-half and twelve years. Her Spelling Age, at seven years is extremely poor and Reading Accuracy at the eight year level is very much below what we should expect. Comprehension, at the nine-and-a-half year level is below expectations, but is the best she could score as the accuracy of her reading was not sufficiently good for her to complete the Neale Analysis Test.

mΧLaGoW∫ i∫ f⁴WⱩ Ca h∫m d C| Ø t∫
My   Lego   is funny 'cause you can make   lots

Fʊ F인G∫ mΧⅅîΧน∫orⱱ i∫m ΧFa γⱱⱱ ⁱ
of things.   My dinosaurs   is (are)   my favourite

Ɑ.b Coⱱ Yⱱ(bⱰ Ĉ.7Iⱱγⁱm ⁱⱱ ⁱⱩⱱⱨ Χ ⱳⱭbbⁱ
because   you can colour them   in. It's my Daddy's.....

Handwriting shows poor letter formation, uncertainty about directionality in forming letter shapes, erratic use of capital letters, sequencing errors, reversals and inversions (b/d and n/u), irregular spacing between words, poor understanding of phonic regularities (e.g. vce words) and lack of punctuation.

Wendy is an extremely articulate child to talk to. She is very good at maths, but has had considerable difficulties in learning multiplication tables and in telling the time. Wendy is far from being the worst in the class and fits the picture of the "puzzling, underachieving" child. A look at the home background reveals that Wendy too comes from a stable home with Father and Mother extremely anxious about her lack of achievement in reading and written language. Father reports that he too is a poor speller, and recalls this was a problem for him during his school years. Wendy has an older brother and a sister at the same school, neither of whom appear to be having particular problems. From inspection of Wendy's profile, we have every reason to suspect this child may be dyslexic and should recommend further assessment.

While every case will not be as clear cut as these, if there are any grounds for suspicion, it is best to be cautious and refer the child on for more investigation. The appropriate channels for further assessment and for obtaining advice on remedial programmes have already been set out. Be sure to pass on the details of your own assessment and findings, as it may not be necessary to carry out all the tests again.

The value of criterion-referenced assessment should also be taken into consideration, as this will be important in drawing up a plan for remedial work. In addition to the material produced by the well-known publishers, schools can also devise their own systems for criterion-referenced assessment based on the curriculum as defined by individual school policy. The following is a sample of the type of criterion-referenced material available in schools in my own area of Strathclyde. The materials, known as TIME (Teacher Initiated Monitoring and Evaluation), were produced by Julie McDonald and Michael Harker of Renfrew Division Psychological Service.

RENFREW PSYCHOLOGICAL SERVICE   TEACHER INITIATED MONITORING AND EVALUATION

SEQUENTIAL SKILLS SCHEDULE
READING

Code	Phonic Skills	Errors		Comments
RP1	Repeats letter sounds aloud (indicate errors)	a b c d e f g h i j k l m n o p qu r s t u v w x y z		
RP2	After demo., matches letters from an array of letter cards, when asked to,' give me two the same'.	a b c d e f g h i j k l m n o p qu r s t u v w x y z		
RP3	Points to correct letter when asked to, 'show me the letter which says....'	a b c d e f g h i j k l m n o p qu r s t u v w x y z		
RP4	Reads aloud letter sounds	a b c d e f g h i j k l m n o qu r s t u v w x y z		
RP5	Gives initial sound of objects in picture cards (after correctly naming objects in pictures)	a b c d e f g h i j k l m n o p qu r s t u v w x y z		

Code	Phonic Skills	CAN DO	Errors	Comments
RP6	Reads aloud consonant-vowel blends			
RP7	Reads aloud regular C-V-C words			
RP8	Reads aloud 4 and 5 letter words with double letter endings			
RP9	Reads aloud regular 4 letter words containing final consonant blends			
RP10	Reads aloud regular 4 letter words containing initial consonant blends			
RP11	Reads aloud regular 4 letter words containing final consonant digraphs			
RP12	Reads aloud regular 4 letter words containing initial consonant digraphs			
RP13	Reads aloud word containing common vowel digraphs			

M. E. HARKER AND J. McDONALD

If peripatetic help is to be made available from a specialist teacher of children with SpLD, then the involvement of an educational psychologist will almost inevitably be essential. The psychologist will then be able to confirm the teacher's findings and also obtain a more complete profile of the child's intellectual ability using the Wechsler Intelligence Scale for Children, British Abilities Scales, Stanford-Binet or other similar test. Additional help may either be given within the school situation, or sometimes at a specialist centre. Some areas are not fortunate enough to have specialist help. In these cases, class teachers must do their best to acquire the appropriate skills. For teachers who feel they would like to acquire more specialised knowledge, training courses are available in many areas. (Appendix 5 gives more details)

Parents should of course be involved and kept informed of what is happening with their child at all stages in the process, responsibility for arranging contact with the parents resting primarily with the headteacher. It should be emphasised that the earlier specific learning difficulties are diagnosed, and a programme devised for remediation, the better the prospects of recovery. Even if a child is to receive specialist help, there will probably be a waiting list of pupils and it may be some time before help becomes available from this source. For children whose difficulties are not sufficiently severe for them to merit specialist help or where such help is not available, then the school psychologist will be able to offer advice on how the child's needs can best be met within the classroom situation.

WHAT CAN THE CLASS TEACHER DO TO ALLEVIATE PROBLEMS?

If the child's difficulties are relatively mild, or if he is considered to be working to his intellectual capacity, then he is unlikely to get any form of specialist help from outwith the school. Nonetheless, a well-structured programme is essential if the child's problems are to be minimised. Your school psychologist should be able to give advice in devising this programme for the individual child. If a learning support teacher is available in the school, then valuable help should be available for carrying out the programme. The child who has specific learning difficulties, even though they may be mild, will require the programme to be of a multisensory nature and structured phonically in such a way that any points which the child is unsure of will be covered methodically and thoroughly in a cumulative way. Diagnostic assessment will determine what must be included in the child's programme.

The class teacher can also do a considerable amount to alleviate problems in the classroom. Much can be achieved by adopting a positive outlook towards the child and praising him whenever possible. These children are only too well aware of their own inadequacies and need constant encouragement to build confidence. The following suggestions may help:

- Give credit for oral responses whenever this is feasible.

- Mark written work on content. While you must make it clear that there are spelling errors, do not dwell on this aspect, or the child will become inhibited and unwilling to produce written work. Find other ways of tackling the spelling difficulties. Games and computer work as well as a structured multisensory spelling programme will be more effective than red ink. See Appendices 2 and 3 for suggestions on materials.

- If you give set homework, find out how long this takes the child to complete at home, and adjust the amount accordingly so that it can be completed in a reasonable time according to the child's age. Dyslexic children may take hours to complete work which would take others ten minutes.

- Seat the child in a position where you can give help easily, but without embarrassing him. Make sure he is facing the blackboard, as he may become easily disorientated by having to turn round.

- Allow the child to make use of a tape recorder whenever this is feasible. This will give the child confidence in using the machine and can be used to record answers orally if written work is liable to be illegible or difficult to understand. A quiet corner of the classroom will be necessary for this type of work.

- Allow the child extra time to copy work from the blackboard or book. With older children, it may be best to provide a neat copy or a photocopy, if insufficient time is available or if efforts prove to be indecipherable.

- If the child is unhappy about reading aloud in the class, don't ask him to. Allow the child to join an appropriate group for discussion when this is feasible. Even though written work or reading may not be up to the standard of the higher group, the dyslexic child will be motivated by being included in discussions which are more suitable for his intellectual level.

- Give practice with alphabet sequencing and dictionary skills. Throughout life, the use of a dictionary will probably prove to be necessary. Therefore, as soon as the child knows the sequence of the letters in the alphabet, he should practise his skills in using the dictionary. Again, this can be tackled as a group activity, as there are always a number of children in any class who will benefit from such training. Teach these children to divide the alphabet into quartiles.

The four quartiles are found by dividing each half of the dictionary. The pupil should learn that by halving the dictionary, he will open it around the letter M. By further halving it, he will arrive around D in the first half, or S in the second half. Games are often helpful to give reinforcement.

- While individual help for a sustained period of time is not always possible in the classroom situation, try to give a few minutes regularly throughout the day to ensure the child is succeeding at least in some of the work. Where it is not possible to give as much attention as the child needs, consider using the same structured multisensory programme for other types of learning difficulties and form a group for this type of teaching. (See page 20). In this situation, groupings have to be flexible as the child will probably be better in a different group for areas of the curriculum not affected by his specific difficulties.

- Organisational skills are very often weak, and it will help if the teacher can suggest ways of helping. Primary teachers, for example can get the whole class to make a note in homework jotters that the next day is a gym day and that they must bring their kit. This way, parents will probably see it and make sure that they remember to put their kit in their bags.

For secondary children, they must have multiple copies of their timetable, so that if one gets lost or mislaid, they always have a spare copy. They must keep a copy in a sensible place, such as a Homework Notebook where it can be readily consulted. They must know where to find a spare copy if the first gets lost.

Parents can help here too by having a large copy of the child's timetable mounted on the child's bedroom wall where it can be consulted each night so that the child always puts the necessary books and kit in his bag for the next day. Having everything labelled with the child's name, class and home address may seem an obvious precaution, but for the child who is liable to mislay things, it is really a basic essential.

- Start training the child on memory skills if this is an area of weakness. See later section on Memory.

WHAT ARE STRUCTURED CUMULATIVE MULTISENSORY METHODS?

The primary sensory systems concerned with language perception and development are the auditory, visual and tactile- kinaesthetic. A problem in these sensory systems may cause specific language difficulties, with subsequent problems in learning and blending sounds and in the sequencing of phonic units. Thus neither a "look-and-say" nor a "phonic" approach will succeed on its own or even in combination. However, success can be achieved when there is coordinated interaction of all the requisite senses: when the pupil sees, hears, writes and speaks simultaneously. This "multisensory" learning then integrates the visual, auditory, kinaesthetic and oral capabilities of the pupil and encourages the use of the child's strengths, while at the same time exercising the weak areas. For example, when a child is learning the letter "d", he will listen to the teacher say the letter name and the sound /d/. He will look at it, say the letter name and the sound, and he will practise writing the letter on various surfaces. Once the child is ready, he will use a very similar procedure in learning to spell words. It is necessary to build the child's knowledge one small step at a time. For this reason, the teacher has to be quite sure what the child really knows, and structure the teaching in such a way that the child will build his knowledge in a cumulative way, firmly basing new knowledge on that which has been acquired. The child then progresses in a clearly devised order. It is of course necessary to record the child's progress methodically, so that it is plain for all concerned in the child's programme exactly where he is at any point in time.

MEETING THE CHILD'S SPECIFIC NEEDS IN VARIOUS AREAS OF THE CURRICULUM

In addition to the general help recommended earlier, the child requires a specific individualised programme to meet his needs. It is appreciated that in the classroom situation, there may not be sufficient time to cope with a number of individual programmes for children with differing difficulties. With due consideration however, it should be possible to organise groups in a flexible enough way that such children can work to their capacity alongside others who may have similar types of difficulties, but for different reasons: for example - children for whom English is not their first language, or children with more general learning difficulties. A bright dyslexic child may not like to be categorised in such a way. If however the organisation is sufficiently flexible, the child can be in different groups at different times for different areas of the curriculum. While this is commonplace in the majority of classrooms, it is worth considering that many children with difficulties will find structured multisensory methods an invaluable aid to the learning process.

SPECIFIC HELP IN VARIOUS AREAS OF THE CURRICULUM

The following is a very brief selection of ideas which a teacher can use to help children with specific learning difficulties to cope with the everyday curriculum. It also gives an indication of the areas which are likely to be implicated. It must be stated that overlearning is necessary and much is left to the ingenuity of classroom teachers to devise strategies and techniques involving the overlearning principle, which will interest and motivate particular pupils.

LANGUAGE WORK

Reading

For the majority of children, the achievement of reading skills represents additional access to education. Much of their future learning will be determined by the level of their reading achievement. The world of books will help the child accumulate information, enlighten existing knowledge, and help him discover his social and cultural background. In the early stages, reading will contribute to the further development of language. Through the related skills of handwriting and spelling he will acquire the ability to communicate and express himself in written language.

For most children, reading is an easier process to master than spelling. This may be due to the fact that reading only requires the child to use recognition processes, as opposed to total recall of words. For reading, it is sufficient for the child merely to recognise the word. He does not have to recall actual letters. In reading, intelligent use of context is often helpful. This is not always the case in spelling. In reading too, there is no necessity to remember patterns requiring motor skill, as is required in writing out spellings. When a child who is otherwise normal in his development fails to learn to read, it is a matter of considerable concern to both parents and teachers alike. What is required is a critical appraisal of why the methods already tried have proved a failure for such children.

Most present reading schemes are based on a combined "look-and-say" and phonic programme. Many children with specific learning difficulties do succeed in achieving a reasonable degree of proficiency using this approach if they are of good ability level. These children are generally relying on areas of strength to compensate for the weaker areas. For example, the child who is a good visualiser may achieve success through recognition of word shapes and patterns, and also may be able to make use of context clues. The child who has poor visual memory, but is good at "sounding out", may also achieve a relative amount of success through his ability to memorise sounds auditorily. When unable to "sound out", he too will make use of context. These children seldom however reach a level commensurate with their ability, and reading is often seen as a chore to be tolerated in the school context, but seldom enjoyed. We have to recognise that the skill of reading is a highly complex mental process, involving not only the recognition of letters and patterns, but also the interaction of context and meaning with visual and auditory information.

A dyslexic pupil needs a structured, cumulative approach in which reading, writing and spelling are integrated. Reading skill is gained by systematically building up letter sounds into syllables, then into words. From words, the child progresses to sentences and to continuous prose. Practice must be frequent and regular. Materials used must be structured in such a way that the child can progress in a logical, step-by- step fashion with continuous monitoring of progress. An excellent example of suitably structured material would be the Letterland system by Lyn Wendon. Other suggestions for useful materials are made in the Appendices at the end. The Alpha to Omega material by Bevé Hornsby and Frula Shear is particularly helpful for the older child, or perhaps for children who have already covered the Letterland material at the infant stage, but still need further help. In cases such as these, there is nothing to prevent teachers from amalgamating from more than one source material: e.g. adopting the mnemonics from Letterland and combining this with a new approach.

The ideas contained in "Learning Difficulties in Reading and Writing - A Teacher's Manual" by Rea Reason and Rene Boote also provide useful ideas for structuring phonic work. The Kathleen Hickey "Multi-sensory Language Course" is excellent, but is probably best left in the hands of the Learning Support specialists as it does require professional training in its use to reach the level of proficiency necessary. The aim of all these methods is to encourage the child to form an automatic response between visually presented letter patterns and units of sound - e.g. "tion" says "sh'n". The child must realise that to sound out individual letters in such cases is of no help in pronouncing a word. With daily practice conducted in a multisensory way, responses should in time become automatic. Stick to around five phonemes at a time until these have been mastered. The more attractive the material presented, the more likely the child is to enjoy what he is doing and to gain maximum benefit from it. For younger children in particular, Letterland provides attractively presented material in a well structured manner, which the children find entertaining and extremely beneficial.

The system introduces pictograms as mapping devices which help children to identify and differentiate between similar letter shapes (b/d/p/q, s/z, u/n, H/N, M/W etc.). Initially the names of the Letterland characters, like the Hairy Hat Man (h), provide a shape/sound mnemonic for each letter, accompanied by a little story explanation.

Reprinted by kind permission of Lyn Wendon

The child then builds on his previously learnt knowledge of single sounds and stories to learn new sounds, such as *sh*. For example, the *sh* story in brief: Sammy Snake (s) loves to hiss, but the Hairy Hat Man (h) hates noise, so the

Hairy Hat Man hushes up Sammy Snake whenever they are next to each other in a word, saying *sh......!* Each story acts as an aide-memoire helping the children to recall pattern, sequence and sound. The examples above show how the children can also 'vitalise' the letters themselves by picture coding them in some words where the sound occurs.

A range of back-up material, including computer software and taped songs, is available and is very useful. Using a progress chart (see illustration), the class teacher can highlight the sounds which the child is unsure of, and structure a programme of work to ensure that these are covered in a methodical, cumulative multisensory way.

	WITCH AT WORK						air, ear, eer	oar, our, oor	PREFIXES	SUFFIXES			
ir	aw	au	ew	ow	ou				re pro	ous	ture	tion	ible etc.

Illustrations by kind permission of Lyn Wendon.

The Alpha to Omega material also offers the class teacher a useful structure with which to work. A set of flashcards are available and offer reinforcement for the multisensory work being done in the programme. The accompanying

Activity Packs give the class teacher some useful backup material without the necessity of having to produce all her own worksheets.

The main problem which has to be faced is how such schemes can be operated within the classroom situation, when the rest of the class have reached the point when they no longer require specific phonic training. Looking at the situation realistically, it will be difficult for the class teacher to find the necessary time to spend practising with one individual, unless some extra provision is made for this. We have to look at the possibilities for employing a strategy which will suit a group either within the classroom, or if this is not feasible, a group comprising children with similar difficulties from different classes could be organised. This is obviously much easier to arrange on a regular basis where a learning support teacher is involved. In grouping children, we must bear in mind the fact that the dyslexic child's problems are primarily in processing symbolic information and not due to lack of intelligence. If the child is grouped with children who have more general learning difficulties for phonic work, he will feel very much aware of this fact, so make sure he is placed with children of his own ability level for other areas of the curriculum.

Once the child is progressing through the phonemes, he should be taught syllabification and learn how to break words into their constituent parts. This will aid both reading and spelling. Affixes should be taught as such and the child encouraged to consider which part of a word is the root, the prefix or the suffix. Bright children may also be interested in the derivation of the various parts of a word.

In teaching word attack skills then, the following pattern should ensure an adequate progression provided the child has adequate experience of all the processes:

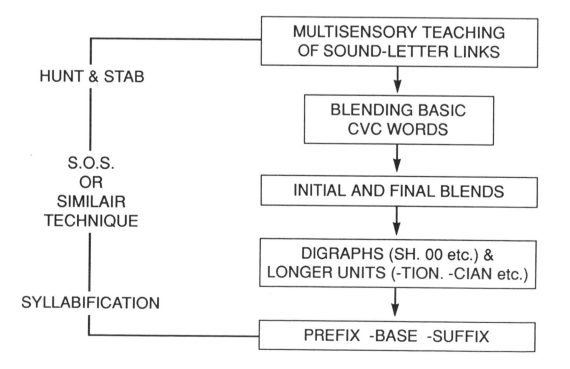

In the case of difficult and irregular words, where these can readily be matched to pictures, matching games, like Pelmanism can be played. Another technique for recognition and recall of irregular words could be through using a Hunt and Stab technique:

1. Choose the necessary irregular words (e.g. from a page of the child's reading book).

2. Put each of the words on a separate, small card and read the words along with the child.

3. Ask the child to identify a specific word. e.g. "See if you can find me the word, *enough*". (Encourage the child to look at initial letters where this will help.) *HUNT AND STAB !*

4. Form the words into a column, and invite the child to try to remember each one.

5. Make a separate column of all the words remembered and congratulate the child on these.

This technique will help the child recognise the words but will probably have very little "carry over" to spelling. For this, and for the remaining words which are posing a recognition problem for the child, we would do better to employ the S.O.S. technique described in the Spelling section.

Encourage the child to look for patterns in a word and show how he can use this to help work out how to pronounce the word. This is necessary for the child to be able to divide words into syllables to aid his word recognition skills: e.g. In the word rabbit, the child should learn to divide the word between the two "b"s in such a way that he will recognise that he has two closed syllables and hence two short vowels (rab / bit). Similarly the child should look out for regular final syllables, such as "ble", "stle", "tion" etc.

In a holistic model of reading, there can be no one method of instruction but a selection of means to achieve the ends. While structured multisensory practice of phonemes on a daily basis will help give instant recognition of letter patterns, the child can also gain much from having stories read. Also, listening to taped books, while at the same time following the story, is useful.

Paired reading either with a good reader or with parents can be encouraged to give the child much of the pleasure of books which he is losing through his difficulties. There is a great deal of evidence that the involvement of parents in both *paired* and *shared* reading can be highly beneficial.

To help the child to "sound out" words he is unsure of, he must be taught how to break words into their constituent parts. In multisyllabic words the child should be encouraged to consider which part of a word is the root, the prefix or the suffix. The child of normal intelligence will readily adopt the use of such terms. The ideas imbued in the Breakthrough to Literacy programme might be found useful, but bear in mind the level that the child has reached in the structured programme and gear the work to match.

There is significant research evidence which suggests that training children to recognise alliteration and rhyme will help them develop reading and spelling skills. It is therefore useful to encourage all children to be aware of these features of language from an early age. To establish any children who may lack awareness of alliteration and rhyme, invite them to find words which start with the same letter : e.g. clever, cunning, cool, ... cat. Children find as many words as possible. The same applies for rhyming words : my, fly, sly,... spy. Children can also be asked to pick out a word which **doesn't** rhyme from a rhyming series. The programme can be implemented using a games approach which the children will enjoy. The whole process can be made more multisensory using plastic or wooden letters so that children can learn to recognise the patterns in words by exchanging a letter or two : e.g. pin, win, fin, spin. These ideas are developed more fully in Lynette Bradley's booklet on "Assessing Reading Difficulties". See Appendix.

In all activities connected to the reading process, adequate practice is vital to develop efficient memorisation and automatisation. At all times due regard must be given to what is going on within the learner. For this reason he must be motivated by the self-improving and self-rewarding nature of reading. It is critical therefore that the teacher accept responsibility for providing the child with material which is at an appropriate level and stage for his individual needs. Some suggestions are made in Appendix 2 for material which can be used with children with specific difficulties and also for older dyslexics who would be insulted by the initial stages of infant reading schemes. At all stages, the teacher must be guided by the child If a child dislikes a series of books sufficiently, he is unlikely to learn much from them. Try to find a series which appeals, and then encourage activities which will sustain interest level throughout.

Once the child is reading at a reasonably efficient level, the aim will be to improve *speed and accuracy*. There are different ways of doing this : e.g.

1. Computer programs can be motivating and may help build up confidence.

2. Kathleen Hickey, in her book "Dyslexia: A Language Training Course for Teachers and Learners" suggests letting the child tape-record himself reading a familiar passage. To avoid damaging the book, place an acetate sheet over the page for the child to mark. When the child has finished reading, he plays the passage back to himself following carefully in his reading book with the point of a marking pencil under the words.

If he has made a mistake, he underlines the word. He then rewinds the tape and plays it back, again following carefully. When he comes to the wrongly pronounced word, he starts taping again, pronouncing the word correctly, and continues reading while taping the rest of the story. He is aiming to complete the passage more quickly than on the previous attempt.

When he finishes taping his reading for the second time, he presses STOP, then PLAY, making sure the volume is turned up. If he can still hear his own voice, then he can feel satisfied that he has improved both his speed and his accuracy. He can do this a few times until he is satisfied that he has no more mistakes. The teacher will of course have to supervise that he is able to spot his mistakes.

3. Many dyslexic children read the little words wrongly, even when they have reached a stage when they are getting the bigger words correct. This is often due to concentrating hard on the larger words at the expense of the smaller ones. To improve accuracy, Hickey suggests marking a passage that the child is reading, telling him that he has around ten points to start with. Every time he makes a mistake with a little word like "a", "the", or "of", he loses a point.

Make this type of exercise fun. Two children with similar difficulties can try to spot one another's mistakes. Do not worry about the bigger words in this instance and mark only the little words which the child knows he should be getting right. The child aims to achieve a higher score each time he reads a page of equivalent length.

Spelling

Spelling is the tool of writing. The purpose of children being taught to spell is that they may become fluent in written language. The goal in teaching spelling is therefore not for belaboured accuracy, but to encourage spelling to become an automatic process. When children have specific learning difficulties, the acquisition of spelling patterns in response to spoken language does not take place as a matter of course. Considerable effort on the part of both the teacher and the learner is required, and much overlearning on the part of the child must take place before a word will become known. When specific difficulties are severe, I think that we must accept the fact that our children may never become perfect at spelling on every occasion. Our aim for these children is to give them spelling strategies which will enable fluency in writing words, and sufficiently logical spelling that their work will be easily understood by all who read it. In teaching spelling, multisensory methods are again advocated.

The child should hear the sound or word he has to spell, say the sound or word, spell it, write it, look at it and check his spelling. The technique for S.O.S. described later in this section employs multisensory methods in this way. The Look, Cover, Write and Check routine is also described and can be used in a multisensory way. For a child who has normal intellectual ability, there is absolutely no reason why spelling rules should not be taught. In fact, it is advocated that they should be. To do this, the class teacher has to make sure she is acquainted with these herself before teaching them to the children. Books such as "Logical Spelling", "Exercise Your Spelling" etc. set out spelling rules quite methodically. We must of course follow an extremely logical structure if we are to cover all the main rules, and we must record the child's progress so that we know exactly what has been taught and when, so that any other teacher can take over if necessary and complete the programme. Ideally, we would follow a similar structure for spelling to that in use for phonics. If spelling is practised and tested daily, this encourages spelling to become the automatic process for which we are aiming. Spelling should follow the sequence of:

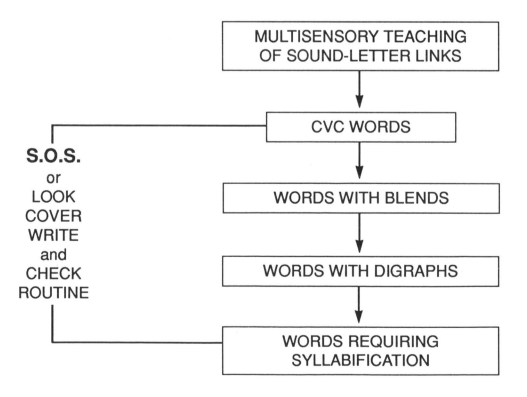

Teach:

1. Groups of words which rhyme:
e.g. send, mend, spend.

2. Sound patterns and digraphs:
e.g. ee, al, est, igh.

3. Rules, guidelines and regularities.

Where no actual rule may apply, the child has to learn to use appropriate guidelines, such as "The first choice for an /ē/ sound in the middle of a one-syllable word is ee ". Where this will not always give the right spelling, it gives the most likely.

4. Alongside enabling the child to relate spelling patterns to sounds, much rich information can be gained from discussing derivations, functions and meanings of words. Looking at the roots of words can enable the child to see why homonyms are represented differently in spelling: e.g. "threw" and "through".

Prefixes and suffixes should be considered for the meaning which is conveyed through them. Instead of regarding English words as "just plain stupid", the child will see the logic of spelling words differently to differentiate meaning. For the older child, recognising the relationships between words such as "statistician" and "statistics" will help the child realise why we do not use the spelling "statistition". Unless the help of a learning support teacher is available on a daily or near-daily basis, it may well be difficult for a class teacher to justify the time to spend with one individual child. It may however be quite conceivable to establish a group who would benefit from such methods. This may or may not be the same group as for reading. Examples of suitable schemes for spelling are suggested in Appendix 2.

Lynette Bradley's *Simultaneous Oral Spelling* technique (S.O.S.), first described by Gillingham and Stillman, is multisensory and has proved highly successful. The procedure for this is:

1. Words to be learned are presented one at a time, each on a small card. (Alternatively, make up the word with the child, using wooden or plastic letters.)

2. The teacher reads the word and the child repeats it.

3. The child then writes the word saying the name of each letter as it is written, repeating the word.

4. The child then checks back to the original to see if the word is correct.

5. The word is covered, and the process is repeated twice more.

If the word is practised three times a day for five or six days using this technique, it may well succeed when other methods have failed. To reduce the load on memory the word should be related to others which have the same pattern and sound.

The *LOOK, COVER, WRITE and CHECK* routine is very similar and is the method advocated by Charles Cripps. To gain maximum benefit, the child requires to attend to a few additional factors when employing this technique.

LOOK: The child should say out the spelling of the word while at the same time looking at it. He may require to spell out several times while at the same time trying to visualise the pattern. Only when he thinks that he can remember the word, should he continue to the next stage.

COVER: The word is covered so it cannot be seen.

WRITE: The word is then written from memory, again saying the spelling while writing.

CHECK: Check carefully by spelling out the original while looking at both the original and the written version. If the word is wrong, go back and repeat the process.

The word should be practised a few times and the child should come back to it again at regular intervals until the word is really known.

Whatever the age or stage of the child the emphasis is, as always, on the use of multisensory methods when practising spelling and also in building up the child's spelling vocabulary in a structured and cumulative manner. While explaining the logic behind spelling will help, it is insufficient on its own. The essentials when practising spelling words are that the child must see the word, say the word, hear the word, spell out the letters in the word, then look and check that the word is correct. He must learn to monitor his own spelling and look carefully for any mistakes, so that constant dependence on the teacher will gradually diminish.

Dictionary use should be encouraged too, but not always when the child is in the process of story writing, as this may inhibit the flow of writing. In this case it may be better to come back at the end of the story, and check through, looking out for doubtful words and checking with the dictionary. If the child is still making huge numbers of spelling errors, then it would be sufficient for him to check out just a few of the most common mistakes. It is a good idea for the child to make his own pocket-size dictionary of words which he frequently misspells, so that he can consult it regularly to check his spelling, or add to a pocket-size list such as Eileen Stirling's Checklist. If the child is unable to spot any likely mistakes on his own, then he may need a little guidance. Examples of the type of dictionaries which may be suitable for children with SpLD are given in Appendix 2. It is for the teacher to provide alternatives and for the child to decide which he finds most suitable.

Correcting spelling

When the child is satisfied with his efforts, the teacher can then go over the work with him. In correcting the child's work, it is far better not to mark over his writing. It is less demoralising for the child if we have a system of writing the word correctly in the margin and allow the child to go over and correct the mistakes himself.

When formal spelling is given, the teacher must decide the appropriate number of words to be practised at a time. For the younger child three or four are likely to be sufficient. Words with the same phonic point can be taught as a group or family. Words which have similar sounds but which do not follow the rule being taught, should be treated as irregular words e.g. when teaching the rule that "ll" is used for an /l/ sound at the end of a one syllable word after a short vowel, teach the word "pal" as irregular. The child can then practise that word using the multisensory technique described before. When setting spelling homework for children with specific learning difficulties, it is best to set only words which have previously been taught or for which the particular phonic point has been taught. Homework is then being used as a technique for reinforcement of the teaching points. It should not be a substitute.

When testing words to establish if the child has retained them, check that the child also knows the meaning. This is especially important if the word is a homonym. It is a good idea always to use the word in a sentence, so that there is no doubt as to what you mean. A sentence or two for dictation is recommended to give the child further reinforcement using the word in its appropriate sense. Sentences should however be matched for phonetic content with the pupil's ability level, and fitted to the cumulative programme. Spelling and sound patterns which have not been taught should not be included. Silly or ridiculous sentences e.g. "A bright light might give me a slight fright at night." can be used to emphasise a specific (in this case, rhyming) pattern and often act as better aids to memory, than conventional examples. Increase the length of the sentences gradually as the child progresses. In this way the child's working memory span can be expanded. Encourage the child always to repeat the sentence or part of sentence before writing it, so that both you and he can ensure it is correct. The use of mnemonic strategies as an aide-memoire is often effective for the child who is unable to visualise the pattern of a word, but has sufficient auditory memory skill to memorise mnemonics. The more ridiculous the mnemonics, the more likely they are to be remembered e.g. "Some Nuns Run Very Well" may help a child to remember when to use "el" instead of "le" at the end of words after s,n,r,v and w - tunnel, not tunnle. This in addition to a pictorial representation may be even more useful: e.g.

"a MAN with too MANY heads"   "a CLOWN with a FROWN and a CROWN"

Children can be very good at thinking up their own mnemonic strategies if encouraged to do so. If they put their drawings and spellings onto a pack of small cards, both teacher and pupil can see the reasoning behind the strategy and ensure that this is sound.

Handwriting

The teaching of handwriting should accompany the teaching of a phoneme. Therefore when teaching a single letter sound or pattern of letters, the child should be encouraged to write the appropriate letter or letters while simultaneously learning the sound. As soon as the child is able to write the correct letter shape, it is appropriate to teach an appropriate cursive style of handwriting. An "appropriate style" would be one which is very similar to the school's own, but with the necessary joining strokes added. The examples which follow show lower case letters which include the necessary ligatures to enable the child to join every letter in a word. Capital letters would not join.

Aa Bb Cc Dd Ee Ff
Gg Hh Ii Jj Kk Ll
Mm Nn Oo Pp Qq Rr
Ss Tt Uu Vv Ww Xx
Yy Zz or y.

Reasons for using a cursive style with dyslexic children are:

1. to encourage a left-right progression.

2. to eliminate uncertainty over where to start the different letters

3. to increase the child's confidence by joining all the lower case letters

4. to avoid confusion of the "ball and stick" letters: e.g. *b*, *d*, *p* and *q* are less easily confused than b, d, p and q.

5. to encourage correct placement and sizing of letters: e.g. *splint* is better written than *splint* .

6. to try to eliminate the use of capitals within words.

7. to reduce spacing problems between words.

8. to eliminate the necessity of switching from one visual/sound form to another at a later stage so that the written response is automatic.

9. to encourage the natural flow of sound into shape through the movement of the hand.

10. to encourage the child to use digraphs as one unit of sound.

11. to encourage the writing of irregular words to become an automatic response.

12. to develop a flowing, reasonably swift style of handwriting and reduce the amount of time taken.

There may be a few problems to begin with in linking the visual image which the child sees on notice boards and books to that which he has to write. This is something which the child will overcome through practice and will have to overcome at some stage anyway whether or not he uses a fully cursive style. The main advantage is that the uncertainty as to where to start and "Do I join this one or not?" will be gone.

All letters should be referred to by their names as well as their sounds.

For children who are completely lacking in pencil control, additional practice may be given through prehandwriting exercises, such as those of Nelson.

Procedure for handwriting a phoneme

A procedure for introducing and practising a phoneme for handwriting would be:

(a) Teacher writes the capital letter on the board and names it, then gives the sound: e.g. writes B - says "bee", then says sound "/b/".

(b) Teacher prints the lower case letter, shows how approach stroke and carry-on stroke are added, then goes over the whole letter.

(c) Teacher writes and names the letter in cursive form, then says the sound.

(d) Child traces over the letter with finger saying both name and sound.

(e) Child takes chalk in dominant hand, rests other hand on top, says letter name and sound and repeats the process several times. This can be done until the teacher is satisfied that the child has the "feel" of the letter and can match letter and sound. The child can also practise writing the letter in the air using a whole arm movement while simultaneously naming the letter and sound. Asking the child to write the letter on the blackboard with eyes shut forces him to concentrate his efforts on the hand and arm movements necessary to produce the letter. This gives additional input and is a useful exercise while at the same time introducing an element of fun.

In the case of a digraph, such as "sh", the same procedure would be adopted, the child saying both letters "ess, aitch", followed by the sound "/sh/".

From here the child progresses to writing the letter/s in his jotter, firstly alone, then as part of a word, and then in a sentence. A comfortable seating position should always be adopted and the angle of the child's jotter will depend on whether he is left or right handed.

Position for right hander   Position for left hander

The use of lined paper is recommended if the child has difficulty writing in a straight line. This also helps with positioning of letters and spacing between lines. Tramline paper is available from suppliers such as Philip and Tacey and is useful for guidance in the early stages of handwriting or where difficulty persists. See Appendix 2 under Handwriting. If the child requires to include drawings as part of the written work, then a jotter with one page lined and one page blank will be of use. Alternatively a sheet with heavily marked lines can be placed under the blank page so that the child can see the lines underneath to give guidance.

If the child has a wrong or poor grip of the pencil, a pencil grip (available from the majority of educational suppliers) may well prove useful. For older children who would be embarrassed by using a grip, but still need to correct their pencil hold, three-sided pencils (available from L.D.A.) often prove successful.

Continuous Prose Writing

The writing of continuous prose is a step which follows on from the ability to read, write and spell. As these improve, the ability to produce acceptable prose should also get better. The writing of prose however involves the interaction of all the skills the child has been learning. For a story to make sense the child's working memory will have to operate at an acceptable level. As working memory is generally an area of weakness in the initial stages of training, memory exercises to increase the working memory span should be beneficial. (See later section on Memory)

The child has to be able to think up what he wishes to say, put his idea into a sentence and retain it for long enough to set it down on paper. This can be a task of considerable difficulty to the dyslexic child as the sequence of the sentence or indeed the whole sequence of the story can become jumbled as he tries to think of spelling, punctuation and all the other necessary skills involved in writing continuous prose. This is one reason for not putting too much pressure on the child to spell or punctuate accurately.

We do not want to inhibit the flow of words or the creative development of a storyline by constant worry over the technical aspects of writing. These can be improved by encouraging the child to self-correct his work when he has finished. Train him to look over his work critically and try to spot any errors. He can mark his own corrections in the space above where he spots a mistake. The teacher can then see which errors are being spotted and which ones have been missed. If the work is for something important, a redraft can be done. Do not expect even the redraft to be error free in the initial stages, as even copying from corrections is a skill which has to be developed for many of these children. When working memory skills are weak, the child may not be able to retain the correct spelling pattern for long enough to transcribe it correctly or it may become jumbled in the process of transcription.

To avoid the necessity for redrafting pieces of written prose, *word processors* are invaluable. Although in the early stages, the word processor should not be used as a substitute for practising handwriting skills, a word processing program can act as a motivator in the creative writing process. The appearance of the work improves greatly and the child no longer has to concentrate on the physical skill of handwriting. Spelling too seems to improve when the child sees the image on the screen. Although initial progress with the word processor may be slow, once the child becomes proficient in the use of the keyboard, he will soon become more fluent and the necessity for completely redrafting work is eliminated.

Spelling can be greatly improved by the use of the facility to check spelling included in most wordprocessors. The child will then be aware of which words to leave alone. A dyslexic child can often look at a word which is spelled correctly and wonder whether or not it is wrong. The spell-checking facility, through highlighting incorrect words and providing likely alternatives and their *correct* spellings, can itself be responsible for an improvement in spelling.

SpLD (Dyslexia) - A Teachers' Guide

The dyslexic child often lacks any kind of structure for his ideas and it helps if he has a specific skeleton structure which he can follow to give order and sequence to stories and descriptive writing. Kathleen Hickey suggests supplying the child with a specific structure which he can follow on all occasions. For example, a possible story structure might consist of:

1. Introduction of important characters.

2. Setting for story- where it takes place.

3. What happens first?

4. The main part of story- the exciting part leading to climax.

5. The solution- how events turn out.

6. The conclusion.

With descriptive writing, it is a good idea to introduce the principle of a Beginning, a Middle and an End. To encourage writing ideas in sequence, initial paragraph headings drafted on scrap paper should bring some order into what might otherwise turn out to be a disjointed piece of work.

While these plans will help ensure correct sequencing, most children will need encouragement to expand their writing, to build up atmosphere and put in the fine detail that is required to form an interesting story or piece of descriptive writing. This can only be achieved gradually and by discussing with the child how he can improve his existing efforts.

With the younger dyslexic child or child with very severe problems who is unable to produce prose writing in an understandable form, it may be best to allow him to produce his story or description as a series of pictures. Divide the page into around six sections, like a cartoon strip and only request that the child writes one sentence about each picture. This will be enough to work on if there are a considerable number of errors. Alternatively, the ideas contained in "The Really Useful Picture Series" from Learning Materials Ltd. provide a similar framework. (see Appendices 2 and 4.) This will be enough to work on if there are a considerable number of errors. Encourage the production of short sentences initially and build on this.

One day Mum took me to the shops. | Tesco's was very busy. | A man nearly knocked Mum over

The man ran out of the shop. | He was a shop lifter. | The police caught him.

Marking

Do not mark work which the child is not expected to amend. It is demoralising for the child to see a large number of corrections on his book and to have no opportunity to better this. It is better to put items which the child is expected to rectify in a margin at the side of the page. Even although the margin may have several marks, once corrected, the child's own efforts still look reasonable. A code can be devised (e.g. Sp. for "spelling of word to be corrected", C for "capital letter needed", F.S. for "full stop required" etc.). This code can be used for the whole class and can be put up on the wall, so all the children can benefit from this system. It is best not to overcorrect. If there are too many points to be attended to, the child will not remember. It is far better to concentrate on a few points, perhaps only on errors of the same type and work on other points at a different stage.

MATHEMATICS

A few children with specific learning difficulties have no associated problems in the mathematical field. However, for the vast majority of dyslexic children there is at least some overlap. This often affects :

- ability to read, and hence understanding of problems

- the learning of number bonds involved in addition and subtraction

- the learning of multiplication tables

- the understanding of concepts involving directionality. Time and spatial concepts can prove difficult.

- sequencing activities. Remembering a sequence such as days in the week, and months in the year can prove difficult.

- orientation. Getting numbers the right way round is sometimes an associated problem: 5 for 2 etc.

- spatial awareness and the ability to correctly position figures on the page and hence get numbers in the right column etc.

- directionality. Confusion can arise through having to process different operations in different directions: starting at the right in addition, subtraction and multiplication, but at the left when dividing.

- visual discrimination resulting in confusion of signs such as +, x .

- mental arithmetic

Because the majority of maths books require a reasonable level of competence in reading even at the early stages, teachers need to be aware that dyslexic children will need extra support to enable them to cope. Worksheets with simple vocabulary will help, provided the teacher is sure the child knows the words. Pairing the child with a good reader can be advantageous provided the good reader is not also doing the work. We must ensure at all costs that the dyslexic child is not held back from advancing his knowledge of mathematical concepts purely because he has poor reading ability.

To establish the main difficulties in mathematical skills, some form of testing is necessary. If the educational psychologist has used the Wechsler Intelligence Scale for Children during assessment, this will give some idea of capacity for mental arithmetic. A number screening test such as Gillham and Hessè Basic Number Screening Test or similar should give a more overall picture of difficulties. For older children Vernon- Miller Graded Arithmetic-Mathematics Test would be more suitable. (See Appendices 1 and 4 for details of these tests.) These can be used in addition to criterion-referenced assessment, but any form of assessment has to be thoroughly and carefully conducted. Difficulties highlighted will have to be investigated further to discover the reasons behind the problems.

Numeracy problems, like language problems lie in putting together the little skills necessary to achieve overall competence. Directional confusion, poor sequencing, working memory weaknesses, spatial awareness, visual perception and literacy skills are all just as important here as they are in language work, with the added complication that computation does not always operate in a left-right progression. There is also the possibility that when adding for example one teacher may start from the top and another from the bottom. For the child who has poor direction sense, this can be even more confusing. Teachers should be aware of this, and if there is not already a specific policy on this, should insist that a whole school shares the same policy, even though it may seem a small matter. To improve directional sense and sequencing ability for number work, Ann Arbor Number Tracking exercises may prove helpful in training the dyslexic child in this area, provided of course it fits in with the school's own policy.

The principles of multisensory teaching which apply to language work also apply to the mathematical field. Progress must be carefully monitored at each stage, checking that a particular concept has been thoroughly mastered before moving on to the next step. A checklist is often the simplest way of doing this, so long as there is space for additional notes to keep track of the exact nature of any difficulties.

An example is given of an initial checklist taken from the TIME assessment material produced by McDonald and Harker of Renfrew Division Psychological Service. A number of other checklists are produced commercially or schools can devise their own lists, bearing in mind that the attainment targets will need to be broken down into sufficiently small steps that they will accurately describe each child and reflect the difficulties which they are experiencing. Columns are ticked when the child has been taught a specific item, whether he can still do it a week later, a month later etc. and when the teacher is satisfied he really knows how to do it consistently.

TIME   ADDITION

		Above	Some Time	Never	ERRORS
AA.1	Combines sets of objects up to 10 in total and states the total	☐	☐	☐	
AA.2	Adds up to totals of 10 (using concrete materials)	☐	☐	☐	
AA.3	Adds up totals of 20 (without carrying; using concrete materials)	☐	☐	☐	
AA.4	Adds up to totals of 50 (without carrying; using concrete materials)	☐	☐	☐	
AA.5	As above but with carrying	☐	☐	☐	
AA.6	Adds up to totals of 200 (no carrying)	☐	☐	☐	
AA.7	As above but with carrying	☐	☐	☐	

For some children with SpLD, the very language and symbolic nature of mathematical material is itself a major problem. For these children, it is necessary to clarify what we mean by the terms we use. Terms, such as "multiply", "divide", "subtraction" etc. may in themselves pose problems which prevent the child from progressing in simple arithmetic skills. When the initial concepts are understood, the symbols and terms we wish the child to know can be put on to cards so that they can be practised. The examples below show cards for "addition" and "greater than", but these can be made up for any of the mathematical language terms we wish the child to master. These should be tailored to the individual child's needs at any one time. They should be built up gradually as the child requires: e.g. "add", and "and" may be sufficient for the child initially, later supplementing this with "find the sum of" etc.

FRONT OF CARD   BACK OF CARD

FRONT OF CARD   BACK OF CARD

Daily practice of the cards by looking at the front, recalling what is written on the back, and checking that they have remembered the various items correctly can be carried out by the child either individually or with a partner. In the same way, "Find the sum of" could be printed on the front of the card and alternatives written on the back alongside the symbol "+", if this would be more useful for the child.

Because of sequencing difficulties, even a child who has mastered his number bonds may still arrive at the wrong answer. In an addition such as

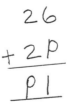

the child knows his number bonds and is saying, "Nine and six is fifteen", but is writing down the one instead of the five, and carrying the five instead of one.

Even more complex sequencing errors are often found. It is well worthwhile asking the child how he arrived at an answer before assuming that he simply cannot do it, or that he is weak in the number bonds. One simple sequencing error may have completely knocked out the whole calculation. When dealing with a problem of this nature, it may be of considerable help to the child if he is allowed to use a jotter with the boxes marked. Encouraging the child to head the columns "Hundreds, Tens, Units", etc. may also help. The child must actively consider that if he has fifteen, he has one ten and five units. The use of concrete material beyond the time when we would expect the child to dispense with this may provide an additional crutch. Often though, the child has understood the concepts, but needs multisensory practice in the sequence of numbers in order that he may write them correctly. If the child practises saying, "fifteen: one ten and five units" as he writes the number, he will learn to think which figure comes first. When doing calculations then, if he first marks his columns with the appropriate headings, the sequence of the numbers should prove easier.

For difficulties with number bonds and tables, many of the same principles apply as have been discussed before. The first step as always is to ensure that the child has a sound understanding of the concepts involved and has had adequate practice using concrete materials and aids: e.g. by sorting activities, one-to-one correspondence, grouping in tens etc. He must also have a sound knowledge of the symbols involved and be encouraged to look at these carefully to ensure he fully understands the nature of the task.

For the child who is a non-starter in recognising and associating symbols with concepts: e.g. who cannot recognise that • • • represents three dots and the symbol "3", sets of wooden or plastic numbers should be used to give the child multisensory practice and to help understanding. Sets are available (see Appendix 4, Westcraft) which have the number of dots etched out on the back of each number so that the child can actually feel the number shape and count at the same time. The technique for practising writing the numbers can be practised similarly to that of the phonemes:

(a) Teacher writes the number on the board and names it: e.g. writes 3 - says "Three" and then draws three dots, saying "One, two, three" as she does so.

(b) Child traces over the number and dots, counting out exactly as the teacher has just done.

(c) Child takes chalk in dominant hand, rests other hand on top and repeats the process several times, until the teacher is happy that the child is confident.

(d) Child then proceeds to writing the number in his jotter in the usual way accompanied by three dots.

There is a considerable amount of structured concrete material available from the educational suppliers to help in understanding place value. It is important for all children to get practice in using this type of material, but it is even more important for children with SpLD as their difficulties in setting down their work and directionality etc. can often be mistaken for lack of understanding. When it has been established that the child understands a concept, any facts we wish memorised can be put on to cards in the way described previously, as remembering may often be a problem for number bonds, multiplication tables etc. Put the problem on one side and the answer on the other, so that the child can practise on his own and self-correct if necessary, the principle again being to add to the cards in a structured cumulative way.

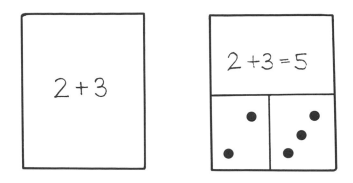

The number of cards which should be added each day should follow the principle of giving the child success as an aid to motivation. If the child sees himself progressing, even if it is only by one number bond or table fact each day, then this is probably more than he has managed previously, and can act as encouragement. If he is pushed too hard, and expected to learn too many facts, he will soon become exasperated and give up trying, exacerbating the problem. He will have to reinforce the facts he has previously learned by a quick "run-through" all his cards each day. If children practise in pairs, it is a good idea to get them to say out the whole bond "3+2=5", rather than just the answer. This gives reinforcement of the whole bond. The child should also be given an opportunity to write these out while saying them, giving true multisensory learning.

If the child cannot be partnered with another who is having difficulties with the number bonds, then again parents may be a useful resource. To avoid this taking excessive time at home, children should only have a few bonds to practise by writing out each night. This will of course include the bond or bonds added that day, and a few others. The bonds not written should be quickly "run through" orally. Parents can also be encouraged to play number games with the children at home. Again we have to be careful that the children know the facts involved in the game, and that the games approach is only used as a reinforcement. If the child is unable to produce the answers fairly readily, he will soon become demotivated even with games.

The tape recording of bonds and multiplication tables is another method of establishing facts which can be made self-correcting, the child being able to work on his own with a minimum of instruction and supervision from the teacher. For example if a group of children are having problems with a particular table, then they can work at a listening bank. The tape has to be made by the teacher to proceed at a pace to suit the children. First the teacher tapes the whole table saying each fact slowly and precisely. Then the teacher records the table, hesitating for a pause before each answer to give the child a chance to "beat the teacher". Then the table is presented in random order, again with the teacher hesitating before giving the answer, allowing sufficient time for the child to think of the answer first.

A further step can be added where the child is asked to write down the fact along with the answer, the teacher providing the answers on a separate sheet for the child to correct later. This ensures that the child does not just cheat and wait for the teacher's answer, although it should be emphasised to him, that as he is not being closely supervised, the only person he can effectively "cheat" is himself. It is best to record each table separately onto a tape of short length (C12 or 15) rather than all on a C90 where the child will have difficulty finding the place. When the child has practised individual tables till he can happily give the answers, he can go on to a tape which contains random examples from the different tables, presented in the different ways.

The use of the computer too is recommended as an incentive to learning for the child who "almost knows" his facts or bonds. Several programs are available which present material in an attractive way. For practice with money, Keyboard Technology have produced overlay contact keyboards using real money keys to give a pleasing and motivating layout. This "Money Box" package allows the child the opportunity to practise addition, subtraction and multiplication of money from the very simplest operations to the more complicated. There is the option to have a printout of the child's achievements so that both teacher and child can see progress being made.

For the child with extremely severe difficulties or for the older child who simply does not have the time to spend on these strategies, without falling further behind, the use of a number square or calculator should be allowed. The argument that if the child uses a calculator, he will never learn the facts is irrelevant. Even if the child has to rely on a prop of this nature for the rest of his life, he should not be deterred from progressing to the next stage in understanding mathematical concepts just because he is unable to rote learn a sequence of bonds or facts.

Many children with specific learning difficulties have difficulty in distinguishing their left from their right. Much practice is necessary with the terms "left", "right", "up", "down", "before", "after", "to", "past" etc. and children can be asked frequently to describe relative positions. A clearly structured sequence of exercises showing progression to enable the child to practise regularly may help a child who is experiencing difficulties with orientation. This will probably start simply with exercises such as "Point to your left ear" and progress through "Touch your right knee with your left hand". The child will finally hope to be able to complete tasks such as "Point to my left ear with your right hand." O'Grady- type games can be used as a fun way of reinforcing orientation skills - e.g. " O'Grady says touch your right knee." "Touch your left shoulder with your right hand." etc. Once it has been established that the child understands the concepts of "to" and "past", and can tell "left" from "right", telling the time can be introduced in the usual order. Introduce multisensory techniques as much as possible. The use of a geared clock is recommended, so that the child can sense the idea of the passage of time while he can at the same time practise saying the time aloud. The idea of self-corrective practice cards described earlier is once again useful in this area to give regular reinforcement without constant teacher supervision.

FRONT OF CARD   BACK OF CARD

Games too, (see Appendix 3) may bring added incentive and motivation to what can otherwise become very tedious but nonetheless necessary reinforcement. Games such as Time Dominoes can both introduce and teach both 12 and 24-hour clocks and give comparisons of analogue and digital times. With adequate teacher supervision, these can be both helpful and effective.

Again if difficulties are affecting older children, it is as well to look at strategies which may circumvent the difficulty. If children require to know the time in order to catch buses to school or to be at certain places on time they can be encouraged to use a digital watch if they can cope with this, rather than persist in trying to learn analogue time. It must of course be ascertained that the child fully understands the relationship between times: that he knows that 10.50 and "ten to eleven" are the same.

Although dyslexic difficulties often affect the child's progress in the field of mathematics they should not be an insuperable obstacle and need not prevent progress. What we must protect against is holding the child back too long because he has not mastered a certain task. It is far better to find a strategy to circumvent the problem, in order that the child can continue to progress with his group, rather than impede his progress unnecessarily.

PHYSICAL EDUCATION

Not all children with specific learning difficulties present a problem in this area, but a fairly large proportion are found to be clumsy and lack motor control. If the children have specific difficulties, even though they may not seem to require extra consideration for physical education, they will generally benefit from a carefully structured programme. These children generally have visual sequencing or auditory sequencing problems which will benefit from a carefully devised schedule in the gym or other suitable space. We must take care however that our intervention is not interfering excessively with the normal development of a child who is happy and enjoys his physical education lessons.

If the child has gross motor problems, the teacher has to be particularly sensitive as the child will very easily become discouraged by lack of ability and may not wish to take part. Alternatively he may present behaviour problems as an avoidance tactic. If dealt with sympathetically however children with gross motor problems and indeed all children with learning difficulties can gain considerably from a carefully planned programme.

Activities must be devised, as with the rest of the teaching, as part of a multisensory programme. One or two periods of physical education per week may not be enough to help the child with specific difficulties. On the contrary these sessions may only serve to reinforce the feelings of failure in front of the peer group. Self-esteem and confidence can consequently be destroyed. Stage by stage progression of a prescriptive type of approach is advised until self-confidence is sufficient for the child to participate with the rest of the class without fear of ridicule. I do not intend going into details of lesson structure, but recommend that teachers should read Jim Russell's book - "Graded Activities for Children with Motor Difficulties". The key to the programme contained in the book is the low level starting points and very gradual progression throughout. The principle is that the teacher selects an appropriate level for the starting activity so that the child will succeed. Progression starts very gradually from this point to harder exercises which will increase the demands on the child.

While this principle could be implemented into any programme of physical education work, the exercises in Jim Russell's book are carefully structured to aid particular areas of weakness and are therefore more appropriate for children with specific difficulties. He recommends teaching in groups of no more than six to allow the teacher to give the required assistance to each child. The activities can however be carried out as a group activity within the normal PE programme.

TOPIC WORK

No special programmes are necessary in this area. It is sufficient to say that the same principles apply to this as to other areas.

Credit can be given for oral responses and the opportunity taken to encourage as much participation as possible. If it is intended to include a significant amount of reading, and the child is still having problems with this, then pair the child with a good reader of similar intellectual ability and allow them to work together.

Also, the reading material available to support topic work should cover the whole range of reading abilities within the class. This includes a number of books which are relatively easy to read and can be used by the children who have specific difficulties. Some suggestions are given in Appendix 2.

THE CREATIVE ARTS

There is absolutely no reason to believe that dyslexic children are in any way different from other children in respect of artistic talent. On the contrary, there is some evidence to suggest that dyslexics are superior on skills such as artistic design and modelling. As one might expect, children with specific learning difficulties may have more trouble in learning musical notation and in reading a score, but eventually, as with reading a book, the skills can be mastered and the child can become extremely successful in this field. Planning may be a problem in such activities, but if the pupil is encouraged to draw up his own timetable and stick to deadlines, he should be able to cope well.

IMPROVING CURRICULUM-SUPPORTIVE SKILLS

MEMORY

In studying profiles of dyslexic children, one aspect stands out as being particularly relevant. While there is a variable pattern of difficulties, one reasonably consistent factor is the very restricted ability which dyslexic children have to use short-term or working memory. An easy assessment of the child's working memory span can be gained by presenting the child with a string of letters or digits at a speed of one per second, and asking the child to recall these. Start with two letters or numbers and increase these one at a time. If a child has a working memory span of only three items, it can be clearly seen why he has difficulty in remembering sequences of letters for spelling and sequences of instructions. The concept of "working" memory should not be confused with "long-term" or "event" memory which are not affected in the dyslexic child. In practice, this means that while the dyslexic can remember every detail of a day-out he had last year, he may not be able to remember three digits in sequence only a few seconds after he has been presented with them. When given sequential instructions, he may only be able to carry out two or three at a time. Working memory however can be improved with training. As in other areas, it is a matter of increasing ability in very small increments.

Increasing the span of items that are to be remembered can be encouraged by getting the child to lay out plastic or wooden letters of the alphabet in an arc in front of him.

The activity of laying out the alphabet in order, may in itself take some time to master, but will prove a worthwhile memory and sequencing exercise. Initially, if two or three children are having difficulty they can be grouped with a better child who can help. Each child should however be given a chance to practise on his own and prove that he can manage it.

To improve auditory skills a sequence of letters is given, starting with around three and aiming to build up to around seven. The pupil listens, repeats the sequence, then pulls the letters out from the arc. The child must learn to use strategies as an aid to memory: e.g. he may group the items in twos or threes. A more difficult task is to present the sequence in jumbled order, but ask the child to display it in alphabetical order. The length of time between presenting the sequence and asking for recall can gradually be increased by about five second intervals. As memory span increases, an intervening task can be given between presentation and recall. With older children who have mastered alphabet sequencing, the plastic or wooden letters can be dispensed with, and the letters written out.

Mnemonic strategies can be encouraged as an aid to remembering sequences of letters, such as "FMPTW" - "Funny Minnie Puts Toys in Wellies." Instead of a sequence of letters, the children can be asked to remember a list of facts or items related to other work in the curriculum. Similar strategies are encouraged. For visual memory, training can be given as before, but this time the items to-be-remembered should be presented visually. The important principle is to ensure that tasks are presented so that success is achieved most of, but not all of, the time. If the child constantly experiences failure, he will quickly cease to enjoy or benefit from such activities.

With young children games will often help. Games such as "I went to the market and bought......." will help auditory sequential memory. Kim's Game in various forms and Pelmanism will help visual memory. The use of gesture as an aid to auditory sequential memory should be encouraged so that each part of the sequence has a specific movement which acts as a memory aid. This is particularly useful for learning poetry or other material which lends itself to forms of dramatisation.

For children having difficulty in learning sequences, such as the months of the year, it may help if they make a set of cards with a visual clue to associate with the month: e.g.

birthday month- April- with a picture of a birthday cake

Christmas- December- with a picture of a Christmas tree

Sequential memory skills can also be improved by adopting a games approach: e.g. the teacher holds up the name of a month and children respond with the one after or before. Children can sequence jumbled cartoon pictures into their right order and then retell the story as it should be.

When using mnemonic strategies as a memory aid, children should be encouraged to think up their own. These can be used to help in all areas of the curriculum. Visualisation techniques will probably help most children. They can be encouraged to imagine whatever they are aiming to remember in larger than life situations. These and other useful memorisation techniques are recommended by Tony Buzan in his books. (See Appendix 6 - Bibliography).

Memory research has shown that the more unusual we imagine an item to be, the more likely we are to remember it. For example, if we wish the child to remember how to spell a word such as "BEAUTIFUL", allow him to devise a mnemonic such as "Big Elephants Are Unusually Timid In Following Useless Lions." The more ridiculous the mnemonic, the more likely it is to be retained. Encourage the use of both mnemonic and visualisation techniques - if possible, both together.

The main point here is that memory can be improved for all children, not just the dyslexic ones. Teaching strategies for memorisation need not be confined to one or two children. Starting points will vary as will increments, but the principles for improving memory can be applied to all.

MOTIVATION

Motivation has been mentioned at various points throughout the booklet. It does however warrant a separate paragraph due to its importance to the learning situation. A child who lacks motivation, dyslexic or not, is unlikely to learn much. It is therefore critical that the dyslexic child, who has probably met failure in much of what he has attempted, be presented with material in such a way that errors and failures are minimised and priority given to maximising his success rate. This will build confidence and encourage the child to persist in tasks which have proved easy for other children of similar intellectual ability. Make use of the child's strengths in order to encourage and exercise the areas of weakness. Praise should be used frequently and opportunities taken to improve the child's self-image and esteem.

On occasions, the child's lack of understanding of his own difficulties will often exacerbate the low esteem and lack of motivation he seems to display. To bring about the desired change in attitude, it is best that someone who understands the child's difficulties fully should explain to him the nature of his dyslexic handicap, and so decrease the fear of "failure". The defensive strategy of "not trying" for fear he might fail will be diminished and seen as unnecessary.

CURRICULAR SUPPORT AT THE SECONDARY STAGE

While the same learning principles apply at the secondary stage as at primary, other difficulties start to present themselves when the child reaches the secondary school. One of these is the problem of having several teachers who all have to be made aware that the child has specific learning difficulties and how this is likely to affect their particular subject area. Another problem for the child is that by the secondary stage, time for the process of remediation starts to run out as important exams loom closer. One means of helping poor readers is to consider the possibility of setting up a paired reading scheme within the school. I know of at least one school where fifth and sixth year pupils are paired with poor readers in first or second year and use their lunch hours to practise. This of course requires a member of staff to organise and monitor, but the amount of supervision required once the scheme is established is minimal. The benefits to the children are considerable and besides the obvious advantages, there is prestige value for first and second year children in having a "pal" in the upper school.

It becomes increasingly necessary to investigate strategies for sidestepping problems rather than expecting each subject teacher to tackle specific programmes within their own area. A number of circumvention strategies, however will probably be required to help the child cope in all the requisite areas of the curriculum. Some points to consider are:

(i) Would the child benefit from having the photocopied notes of the teacher or of a child with no difficulties whose handwriting is also neat and easy to follow? Subject teachers should be able to organise this when it has been approved by the Headteacher.

(ii) Encourage the child to make his own list of vocabulary which he needs to spell for his different subjects along with the meanings of the specific words. A pocket-size notebook clearly labelled with name and class is probably best for this. He can then list his words either by subject title or alphabetically.

(iii) Tape recorders are useful for presenting novels and other material which require a considerable amount of reading. Commercially produced professionally recorded tapes are available for purchase at most major booksellers and most of the popular titles can be bought. For an annual fee, the Calibre Library for the Blind are happy to supply to dyslexic children and they have a huge range of titles available for all age groups.

The tape recorder also offers the child a non-judgmental method of practising his reading aloud.

(iv) Would the use of a word processor help the child get over problems of slow or difficult to read handwriting? Modern wordprocessors can be silent and portable and can be operated with little or no disruption to the class routine. Typing, even badly spelt, is easier for a teacher to mark than poorly formed handwriting which may be difficult, if not impossible, to decipher.

(While it has not yet been established experimentally that spelling actually improves with the use of a wordprocessor, there is some evidence to suggest that the visual image of the word on the screen matching the printed image seen when reading the word in a book helps the child to recognise whether or not the word is correct.) With the majority of wordprocessors which are currently available on the market, it is possible to obtain a facility which will check spelling, and this should help the child to recognise not only the words which are wrong and help with possible corrections, but perhaps more importantly will let the child know which words are likely to be right and should be left alone. Some authorities will supply a wordprocessor for a child who has severe enough difficulties to warrant this, or parents may themselves supply one.

A system is now available for some types of laptop computers which "learns" words as it goes along and stores them in its own dictionary, building up a vocabulary of the words the dyslexic child uses most often. The system, PAL, makes predictions as each letter is typed into the machine. As the child types, the program predicts what the word is likely to be, thus reducing the amount of typing necessary. Using this system, we would also expect a significant improvement in spelling. (See Appendix 2 for further details.)

If it is foreseen that the child will benefit from using a wordprocessor for folio or exam work, then the sooner the child embarks on a programme of keyboard skills the better. The child will probably also require to have regular access to a printer. A member of staff who enjoys computer work and is sympathetic to the child's special needs should take responsibility for helping the child with any difficulties he may have regarding technical difficulties with the machine.

(v) Is the child going to require the use of a scribe or tape recorder in important exams, such as Standard/Higher grades or GCSEs? If so, then it is important that the skills required are practised regularly. In the case of scribing, then nearer to the exam, this practice should be with the person who will be writing in the actual exam.

Is the child going to require extra time or allowances to be made for poor spelling? If so, these must be applied for in good time.

(vi) Coaching in study skills and examination techniques is beneficial to all children, but particularly helpful for dyslexic children who often lack the organisational ability necessary to plan successful programmes of study, and often lack confidence in facing the examination situation. Coaching in time management, note taking for revision, strategies for planning and setting out exam answers, use of a cassette recorder as a method of learning and revision, use of libraries, learning through criticism, the importance of relevance in answering questions, and coping with the fear of failure should all be considered relevant teaching points for the benefit of most, if not all children. There are many books available to give guidance on study skills. Ian Selmes' "Improving Study Skills" is one useful example.

(vii) Children with specific learning difficulties often find the learning of a foreign language quite traumatic, especially if they already have auditory problems or if written work is required. It would seem, however, that languages which are phonically regular and similar in pronunciation to English are easier for the dyslexic child. If a language, such as French, is tackled, then the problems for a child who has not yet mastered English phonics are bound to be considerable. The unknown phonic structure and strange pronunciations are liable to be exacerbated by existing problems. If written work is really necessary then the principles of multisensory teaching should apply. If possible, where the child is having horrendous problems with the written form of the language, I recommend that credit be given purely for oral responses. The child will probably not want to continue studying a foreign language for longer than he can help, but the introduction to the spoken form of the language will be of benefit if he later requires to speak the language.

EPILOGUE

The road to success for dyslexic children is a long and at some points tedious one for all concerned. It cannot be travelled in haste or the child will become lost by the wayside. For the teacher who has the patience to travel at the child's own rate however, the rewards are considerable. To see these children reach their destination, in spite of their adversity, is satisfaction enough.

I hope this booklet has cast some light on the nature of the difficulties encountered by these children and will act as a guide to class teachers on possible directions to follow. No one route is recommended for all. I hope the suggestions contained in this booklet will serve to highlight the possibilities and the most likely channels leading to the desired destination.

APPENDICES

APPENDIX 1 ASSESSMENT MATERIAL

LANGUAGE

AMES, TED, "The Macmillan Diagnostic Reading Pack", NFER-Nelson. (Age level 5-9 years)

ARNOLD, HELEN, "Diagnostic Reading Record", Hodder & Stoughton.

BOOKBINDER, G. E., "The Salford Sentence Reading Test", Hodder & Stoughton. (Quick and easily administered test of reading attainment for Primary School children from around 6 up to a reading age of 10.6.)

BRADLEY, LYNETTE, "Assessing Reading Difficulties", NFER- Nelson.

CLAY, MARIE, "The Early Detection of Reading Difficulties", Heinemann Educational, London. (Intended for selective use with children around their sixth birthday.)

COOPER, M., PARKER, R. & TOOMBS, S., "RAT-Pack: Reading Assessment for Teachers", Wiltshire County Council Education Authority. (For use with Primary Age children with reading difficulties.)

COTTERILL, GILL, "Diagnostic Spelling Tests", Special Educational Needs (Marketing). (A simple means of diagnosing spelling problems at any level between 9 and Adult. Booklet contains practical suggestions as well as the tests.)

DANIELS & DIACK, "The Standard Reading Test", Chatto & Windus. (Suitable for children at Primary School or children with reading difficulties at Secondary. Consult instructions for details of age groups for specific tests.)

JACKSON'S Phonic Skills Tests, "Get Reading Right", Robert Gibson & Sons, Glasgow. (Criterion-referenced Assessment for any age group requiring help with phonics. Has direct application to child's needs and the teaching/learning situation.)

KISPAL, ANNE, ET AL., "Test of Initial Literacy", NFER-Nelson. (Test gives detailed information about the specific problems and abilities of children, who are having more difficulty with reading and written language than would be expected for particular age group. Age 7 + to 12 +).

McCLEOD, J., "GAP Reading Comprehension Test", Heinemann Educational, London. (A cloze comprehension test for Reading Ages 7.8 to 12.0.)

McCLEOD, J., & ANDERSON, J., "GAPADOL Reading Comprehension", Heinemann Educational, London. (Similar to "GAP", but designed to measure levels of reading ability in the Secondary age range, accurate to around 16.)

MILES, T., "The Bangor Dyslexia Test", Learning Development Aids. (Age 7 to adult.)

NEALE, MARIE, "Neale Analysis of Reading Ability - Revised British Edition", NFER-Nelson. (Suitable for children between 5 and 13.)

NEWTON, MARGARET & THOMPSON, MICHAEL, "The Aston Index", Learning Development Aids. (Collection of screening and diagnostic tests suitable for 5-14 year age group).

PETERS, MARGARET L., "Diagnostic and Remedial Spelling Manual", NFER-Nelson. (Graded diagnostic spelling dictations for age range 7 to 12. Manual gives guidelines for improving spelling.)

PUMFREY, P.D., "Reading: Tests and Assessment Techniques", Hodder & Stoughton, London. (Criterion-referenced Assessment.)

QUEST Reading Screening Test, NFER-Nelson. (30 minute test to assess word identification skills and comprehension - suitable for group administration.)

VERNON, P.E., "Graded Word Spelling Test", Hodder & Stoughton. (Age Range 6 to 16+.)

VINCENT, DENIS & CLAYDON, JENNY, "Diagnostic Spelling Test", NFER-Nelson. (A dictation and seven sub-tests to identify poor spellers by examining performance in sub-skills which underlie good spelling, for Spelling Age range 7 yrs. 8 mths. to over 11 yrs. 8 mths.).

VINCENT, DENIS & de la MARE, MICHAEL, "New Macmillan Reading Analysis", NFER-Nelson (Age range 7 to over 11). Suitable for older children with reading difficulties.)

YOUNG,D., "Group Reading Test", Hodder & Stoughton.(Age range 6.5 to 12.10)

YOUNG,D., "SPAR Tests", Hodder & Stoughton. (Tests for Reading and Spelling for Age Range 7 to 12.11.)

MATHEMATICS

GILLHAM, W.E.C., "Basic Number Diagnostic Test", Hodder and Stoughton. (Age Range 5 to 7+.)

GILLHAM, W.E.C. & HESSE, K.A., "Basic Number Screening Test", Hodder & Stoughton. (Age Range 7 to 12.)

LUMB, D. & M., ""Early Mathematics Diagnostic Kit, NFER-Nelson. (4 to 8 years and older children with learning difficulties.)

QUEST Number Screening Test, NFER-Nelson. (Diagnostic test to assess understanding of number concepts - suitable for group administration.

STRONG, R.W. (Somerset LEA), "Assessment in Mathematics", (Organised by sub-skill and topic - for 9 to 14 year olds.)

VERNON, P.E. & MILLER, K.M., "Graded Arithmetic-Mathematics Test", Hodder & Stoughton. (Age Range 5.3 to 18+.)

INTELLIGENCE

BRIMER, M.A. & DUNN, L.M., "English Picture Vocabulary Tests" 1,2 and 3, Education Evaluation Enterprises. (Age Range 5 to 18.)

"MORAY HOUSE TEST OF VERBAL REASONING", Hodder & Stoughton. (Age Range 8.6 to 17.6.)

YOUNG,D., "Non-Reading Intelligence Test", Hodder & Stoughton. (Age Range 6.4 to 10.11+.)

USEFUL BOOKS FOR THE TEACHER

ARNOLD, HELEN, "Listening to Children Reading", Hodder & Stoughton.

BRADLEY, LYNETTE, "Assessing Reading Difficulties: A Diagnostic and Remedial Approach", NFER-Nelson.

COTTERILL, GILL, "Diagnosis in the Classroom", Centre for the Teaching of Reading, University of Reading.

COTTERILL, GILL, "Diagnostic Spelling Tests", Special Educational Needs (Marketing).

DUNCAN, AILEEN & DUNN, WILLIAM, "What Primary Teachers should know about Assessment", Hodder & Stoughton.

LEVEY, BERNARD & BRANWHITE, TONY, "The Precision Phonics Programme", NASEN Enterprises Ltd.

McDONALD, JULIE & HARKER, MICHAEL, "Teacher Initiated Monitoring and Evaluation" (T.I.M.E.), Strathclyde Regional Psychological Service, Renfrew Division.

SPOONCER, FRANK A., "Testing for Teaching", Hodder & Stoughton.

THOMSON, MICHAEL, "Developmental Dyslexia", Whurr Publishers.

VINCENT, D., "Reading Tests in the Classroom: An Introduction", NFER-Nelson, Windsor.

VINCENT, D., GREEN, L., FRANCIS, J. & POWNEY,J., "A Review of Reading Tests", NFER-Nelson.

WEST SUSSEX COUNTY EDUCATION COMMITTEE: PSYCHOLOGICAL SERVICE, "Assessment of Intelligence", West Sussex County Council, available from Education Dept., County Hall, Chichester, West Sussex.

APPENDIX 2 LANGUAGE MATERIALS

Reading

"Bangers and Mash", Longman.

"Breakthrough to Literacy" materials, Longman.

"Chillers", Hodder & Stoughton.

"Code Cracker", Jordanhill Sales and Publications.

"Corrective Reading Series", Science Research Associates.

"Developmental Reading Laboratories", Science Research Associates.

"Fastbacks" (with audio tapes), L.D.A.

"Fat Tom" Series, Emeye Publishing.

"Five Minute Thrillers" (with audio tapes), L.D.A.

"fuzzbuzz", Oxford University Press.

"High Noon Books", Ann Arbor Publishers.

"Jets", A & C Black.

"Letterlinks Early Readers", Letterland Ltd.

"Monster Books", Longman.

"Oxford Junior Readers", Oxford University Press.

"Quest" Workbooks, NFER-Nelson.

"Racing to Read", Series, Thos. Nelson & Sons Ltd.

"Read, Write and Remember" Series, Blackie & Son Ltd.

"Reading for Understanding" Kit, Science Research Associates.

"Rescue Reading" Series, Ginn & Company Ltd.

"Skill Teach: A Structured Reading Resource for Children with Learning Difficulties", PAVIC Publications, Sheffield City Polytechnic.

"Sound Sense" Readers, Thos. Nelson & Sons Ltd.

"Starpol" Series, Ginn & Company Ltd.

"Skyways", Collins.

"Sure Fire Phonics", Thos. Nelson & Sons Ltd.

"The Trog Books", Thos. Nelson & Sons Ltd.

"Tim Books", Thos. Nelson & Sons Ltd.

"Wellington Square", Thos. Nelson & Sons Ltd.

For Topic Work

Easy Reading Editions:

"All Around Us", "Beyond the Classroom", "Introduction to Maps" "Science Series", "The Weather Map" (Expendable workbooks), Learning Materials Ltd.

"Datasearch" (Various titles), Hodder & Stoughton.

"Read, Write and Remember" Topic Books, Blackie & Son Ltd.

Spelling

ALLAN, B. V. "Logical Spelling", Collins Educational.

ALLAN, B. V., "Spelling Patterns", Collins Educational.

ANDERSON, H., "Spelling Books", Collins Educational.

ATKINSON, MARY, "Hear It, See It, Say It, Do It", Emeye Publishing. (contains considerable phonic work and games also.)

BELL, P., "Spelling 1-3", Collins Educational.

BRAND, VIOLET, "Spelling Made Easy" Photocopyable worksheets, Egon Publishers Ltd.

CRIPPS, C., "A Hand for Spelling," Learning Development Aids.

CRIPPS, C., "The Stile Spelling Programme", Learning Development Aids.

DAVIS, G.C., DILLON, S.M. & DILLON, T.D., "Master Your Spelling" Series, Simon & Schuster Education.

DIXON et al., "Spelling Mastery Series", Science Research Associates.

DONCASTER, C.R. & SWEENEY, J.Y., "Key Phonics", Collins Educational.

GREENACRE, IRENE, "Spell-File", (available from Irene Greenacre, "Heathers", Earls Common Road, Stock Green Redditch, Worcs., B96 6SY. Tel. 0386-792543.)

GREGORY, JILL, "Phonics: A Resource Bank for Teachers", Special Educational Needs (Marketing).

GREGORY, O.B. & MAXWELL, C., "Practise Your Spelling", Science Research Associates Ltd.

HUNTER, A. & SUTHERLAND, D., "The Laughing Speller", Blackie.

KING, H., "Learning Sounds - Phonics Kit", NES Arnold.

LEECH, J. & NETTLE, G., "Read, Write and Spell", Better Books.

LEWIS, P., "Spell It", Simon & Schuster Education.

NORRIE, EDITH, "The Edith Norrie Letter Case", from Helen Arkell Dyslexia Centre, Frensham, Farnham, Surrey, GU10 3BW.

PALMER, SUE, "Mind Your Spelling", Oliver & Boyd.

POLLOK, JOY, "Signposts to Spelling", Better Books

PRATLEY, PHIANNEDD, "Spelling It Out", BBC Books, London.

RAK, ELSIE T., "Spellbound", Better Books.

RAK, ELSIE T., "Spellbinding", Better Books.

RAK, ELSIE T., "The Spell of Words", Better Books.

RICHARDS, JEAN, "Attack", P.B.S. Ltd.

RUSSELL, SYLVIA, "Cracker Spell", Jordanhill Sales and Publications.

SADLER, BERNARD, "Spelling Matters", Hodder & Stoughton.

SHEAR, F., RAINES, J., & TARGETT, D., "Space to Spell" & "More Space to Spell", Better Books.

TODD, JOYCE, "Learning to Spell", Blackwell, Oxford.

THOMSON, MICHAEL, "The Book of Letters" and "Word Quest", Learning Development Aids.

WOOD, ELIZABETH, "Exercise Your Spelling" photocopyable worksheets, Hodder & Stoughton.

Handwriting

Exercise Books

PHILIP & TACEY, Special Handwriting Ruling:
                    Primary Ruling 16
                    Cambridge Ruling 15

Handwriting Exercises

NELSON, "New Nelson Handwriting".

Written Language Work

BENTLEY, DIANA, "False Teeth and Vampires", Learning Development Aids.

CLARKE, MURIEL & MARSDEN, FLEUR, "Schoolhouse Word Skills Kit", Science Research Associates.

EVANS, JOY & MOORE, JO ELLEN, "Short Story Sequencing", Evan Moore, Scholastic Publications Ltd.

GROVES, PAUL & GRIMSHAW, NIGEL, "Basic Speech Punctuation", Hodder & Stoughton. (Photocopyable worksheets.)

GROVES, PAUL & GRIMSHAW, NIGEL, "Stops and Starts", Hodder & Stoughton. (Worksheet masters.)

HUTCHISON, LYNN, "Cloze Plus", "Which Word?" and other titles designed to improve comprehension by practice of context and decoding skills. Hodder & Stoughton.

MILBURN, CONSTANCE, "The New Write What You Know", Blackie & Son Ltd.

(LEARNING MATERIALS LTD. have an extensive range of expendable workbooks to help children with writing, language development, listening skills, phonics, mathematics and other skills. Included in this are "The Really Useful Picture Series" and "Picture Writing Books" to help structure creative writing.)

Spelling Dictionaries

FRANKLIN SPELLMASTER, Venture Marketing Ltd., Premiere House, 11-17 Paradise Road, Richmond, Surrey, TW9 1SA. (Electronic spelling aid)

HULME, T.S., CARMODY, T.F. & HULME, J.A., "Black's Writing Dictionary", A & C Black, London. (For Primary and early Secondary age children. Gives simple meanings).

HAWKER, G.T., "Spell It Yourself", Oxford University Press. (Useful for Primary age children).

MAXWELL, CHRISTINE, "The Pergamon Dictionary of Perfect Spelling", S.R.A. (For upper Primary and Secondary).

MOSELY, DAVID & NICOL, CATHERINE, "Aurally Coded English", Learning Development Aids. (Needs some practice to be useful, but some children swear by it!)

STIRLING, EILEEN, "Spelling Check-list: A Dictionary for Dyslexics", Better Books. (Basic list to which children can add their own problem words. Pocket size.)

Computer Software

"AN EYE FOR SPELLING", ESM Software.

"COMPLETE SPELLER", Northern Micromedia. (Suitable for all ages.)

"FLASHWORD", Lander Software. (Designed to reinforce literacy and spelling skills for all levels of ability.)

"ADVANCED FOLIO", ESM Software. (Wordprocessing program offering a professional standard for presentation of work.)

"FUNFAIR", Northern Micromedia. (Basic numeracy skills)

"FUN PHONICS", PAVIC Publications, Sheffield City Polytechnic. (Revision and reinforcement for phonic skills- accompanies Skill Teach Reading Programme.)

"GAMES FOR DYSLEXIC CHILDREN", (BeeDee, City Maze and Doors) I.E.C. Software. (Games to help children with b/d discrimination, left/right and directionality.) Available from Better Books.

"HANDS ON SPELLING", ESM Software.

"HI-SPELL", Suites 1, 2 & 3, Xavier Educational Software Ltd. (A structured approach to learning reading and spelling skills.)

"HOPSCOTCH", Lander Software. (Using a definition printed on the screen , children must identify word to match from a grid. Designed to improve reading and spelling skills.)

"IN A SPIN", Lander Software. (Similar to "Hangman" with a game element.)

"LETTERLAND ON MICRO", Letterland Ltd., Cambridge. (Two software programs for BBC computers.)

"LETTERLAND EARLY AUTHORS", Letterland Ltd., Cambridge. (Software and 26 colourful Concept Keyboard overlays with accompanying audio-cassette.)

"MAGIC E ", Sherston Software.

"PAL", Lander Software. (Used with a wordprocessor, PAL makes predictions as child starts to type each word. Available for PCs & Archimedes/A3000.)

"PALSTAR", Easy-to use wordprocessor comes free with PAL.

"PODD", Available from NES Arnold. (Children can discover 116 actions which Podd can do.)

"PREDICTYPE", Lander Software. (Similar to PAL, but for BBC computer.)

"!PUNCTUATE" Xavier Educational Software Ltd.

"READ RIGHT AWAY" (1, 1A, 2, 2A, 3, 3A, 4), H.S. Software. (Computer-based reading skills programs.)

"!SOAPBOX, SPELLING WITH SPEECH", Xavier Educational Software Ltd.

"STARSPELL PLUS", Fisher-Marriott. (Practice given using the "Look, Cover, Write and Check" routine.)

"!THINKLINK", Xavier Educational Software Ltd.

"VOWELS OF THE EARTH", IEC Software. Available from Better Books.

"WORDWISE PLUS LITERACY PACK", Lander Software. (For the BBC Micro to allow wordprocessing.)

Useful Books for Teachers

ALSTON, JEAN & TAYLOR, JANE, "Handwriting: Theory, Research and Practice", Croom Helm Ltd.

ALSTON, JEAN & TAYLOR, JANE, "Handwriting Helpline", Better Books.

ATKINSON, E.J., GAINS, C.W. & EDWARDS, R. "An A-Z List of Reading Books", Sixth Edition, NASEN Enterprises Ltd.

BENTLEY, D. & KARAVIS, S., "Bright Ideas - Spelling", Scholastic Publications Ltd.

BRAND, VIOLET, "Remedial Spelling", Egon Publishers Ltd.

COTTERILL, GILL, "Teaching the Non-Reading Dyslexic Child", L.D.A.

CRIPPS, CHARLES, "Catchwords. Ideas for Teaching Spelling", Harcourt Brace Jovanovitch Group, Sydney.

CRIPPS, CHARLES, "Joining the ABC", LDA.

CRIPPS, C. & PETERS, M., "Resources for Spelling", Centre for Reading, Reading.

FRITH, UTA, "Cognitive Processes in Spelling", Academic Press.

HEATON, P. & WINTERSON, P., "Dealing with Dyslexia", Better Books.

HERBERT, D. & DAVIS-JONES, G., "A Classroom Index of Phonic Resources", New Extended Edition, NASEN Enterprises Ltd.

HICKEY, KATHLEEN, "The Hickey Multi-sensory Language Course: Second Edition". Edited by Elizabeth Adams, Jean Augur and Susan Briggs, Whurr Publishers Ltd.

HORNSBY, BEVE & SHEAR, FRULA, "Alpha to Omega", Heinemann.

HUNTER-CARSCH, MORAG (Ed.), "The Art of Reading", Blackwell Education.

McDONALD, J. & HARKER, M., "Teacher Initiated Monitoring and Evaluation" (TIME), Strathclyde Regional Psychological Service, Renfrew Division.

McNICHOLAS, JIM & McENTREE, JOE, "Games to Improve Reading Levels", NASEN Enterprises Ltd.

MILES, ELAINE, "The Bangor Dyslexia Teaching System", Whurr Publishers.

MILLAR, ROBIN & KLEIN, CYNTHIA, "Making Sense of Spelling: A Guide to Teaching and Learning How to Spell", Inner London Education Authority.

MOBELY, MAUREEN, "Evaluating Curriculum Materials", Longman.

NASH-WORTHAM, MARY & HUNT, JEAN, "Take Time", The Robinswood Press, Stourbridge.

PETERS, M., "Diagnostic and Remedial Spelling Manual", NFER-Nelson.

POLLOK, J., "Signposts to Spelling", Better Books.

PUMFREY, P.D. & ELLIOTT, C.D., "Children's Difficulties in Reading, Spelling and Writing", Falmer Press (available from Special Educational Needs (Marketing)).

REASON, REA & BOOTE, RENE, "Learning Difficulties in Reading and Writing: A Teacher's Manual", NFER-Nelson.

SCOTTISH COMMITTEE on LANGUAGE ARTS in the PRIMARY SCHOOL, "Hand in Your Writing", Scottish Consultative Council on the Curriculum.

SCOTTISH COMMITTEE on LANGUAGE ARTS in the PRIMARY SCHOOL, "Responding to Children Writing", Scottish Consultative Council on the Curriculum.

SINGLETON, C. (Ed.), "Computers and Literacy Skills", BDA Computer Resource Centre. Available from Better Books Ltd.

SMITH, FRANK, "Reading", Cambridge Educational.

STIRLING, EILEEN, "Help for the Dyslexic Adolescent", Better Books.

TODD, JOYCE, "Learning to Spell: A Resource Book for Teachers", Blackwell, Oxford.

THOMSON, M.E. & WATKINS, E.J., "Dyslexia: A Teaching Handbook", Whurr Publishers Ltd.

WENDON, LYN, "Letterland" Teaching Programs 1 & 2, Letterland Ltd. Cambridge.

WOLFENDALE, S. & TOPPING, K., "Parental Involvement in Children's Reading", Croom Helm.

APPENDIX 3 GAMES

"CLOCK & TIME DOMINOES GAME", NES Arnold. (Helps to teach and consolidate "telling the time" skills.)

GAMES TO "EXERCISE YOUR SPELLING", NES Arnold.

GEARED PLASTIC WORKING CLOCK, NES Arnold.

"LETTERLAND SHUFFLE", Letterland Ltd.

"LETTER SOUNDS GAME", Galt

"PHONIC RUMMY", Better Books.

"PHOTO SOUND LOTTO", L.D.A.

"SOUND LOTTO STORIES", L.D.A.

"SPELLMASTER", Spear's Games. Available from Hope Education.

"SPELLWAY", Spear's Games. Available from Hope Education.

"SPIN-AND-SPELL SPELLING GAME", Philip and Tacey.

"TIME DOMINOES", NES Arnold. (To introduce and teach both 12 and 24-hour clocks and for comparison of analogue and digital times.)

"TIMEWATCH", NES Arnold. (Set of games for consolidation and practice in telling, showing and comparing times.)

"VOWELS AND BLENDS", Taskmaster.

"WHAT'S THE TIME SNAP GAME", Philip & Tacey.

"WORDSPELL", Taskmaster.

APPENDIX 4 USEFUL ADDRESSES

Ann Arbor Publishers
P.O. Box 1
BELFORD
Northumberland
NE70 7JX

AVP (Educational Software)
School Hill Centre
CHEPSTOW
Gwent
NP6 5PH

BBC Enterprises Ltd.
Woodlands, 80 Wood Lane
LONDON
W12 0TT

Better Books and Software Ltd.
3 Paganel Drive
DUDLEY
West Midlands
DY1 4AZ

A. & C. Black
35 Bedford Row
LONDON
WC1R 4JH

Blackie & Son Ltd.   also 7 Leicester Place
FREEPOST   LONDON
Bishopbriggs   WC2H 7BP
GLASGOW
G64 2BR

British Dyslexia Association
98 London Road
READING
Berkshire
RG1 5AU

Calibre Library
(Cassette Library for the Blind and Handicapped)
AYLESBURY
Bucks.
HP20 1HU

Collins Educational
HarperCollins Publishers
Westerhill Road
BISHOPBRIGGS
Glasgow
G64 1BR

Education Evaluation Enterprise
A.W.R.E.
NEWNHAM
Glos.

Egon Publishers Ltd.
Royston Road,
BALDOCK
Herts.
SG7 6NW

Emeye Publishing
4 Plain Tile Cottages
Bird Lane
UPMINSTER
Essex
RM14 1TY

ESM
Duke Street
WISBECH
Cambridgeshire
PE13 2AE

Rbt. Gibson Publisher
17 Fitzroy Place
GLASGOW
G3 7BR

Ginn & Co. Ltd.
18 Bedford Row
LONDON

Heinemann Educational   also 5 March Road
FREEPOST   EDINBURGH
P O Box 381   EH4 0HS
OXFORD
OX2 8BR

Helen Arkell Dyslexia Centre
Frensham
FARNHAM
Surrey
GU10 3BW

Hestair Hope Ltd.
St Philips Drive
Royton
OLDHAM
OL2 6AG

Hodder & Stoughton Ltd.
P.O. Box 6
Mill Road
Dunton Green
SEVENOAKS
Kent
TN13 2YA

HS Software
56 Hendrefoilan Avenue
Sketty
SWANSEA
West Glamorgan
SA2 7NB

I.E.C. Software
77 Orton Lane
Wombourne
WOLVERHAMPTON
WV5 9AP

Keyboard Technology Ltd.
Unit 3, Gordon Road
Meadow Lane Industrial Estate
LOUGHBOROUGH
Leicestershire
LE11 1JX

Lander Software
(Scetlander)
74 Victoria Crescent Road
GLASGOW
G12 9JN

Learning Development Aids(L.D.A.)
Duke Street
WISBECH
Cambs.
PE13 2AE

Learning Materials Ltd.
Remedial Supply Co.
Dixon Street
WOLVERHAMPTON
WV2 2BY

Letterland Ltd.
Barton
CAMBRIDGE
CB3 7AY

Longman
FREEPOST
Longman House
HARLOW
Essex
CM20 2JE

MAPE
Computer Centre
Newman College
Bartley Green
BIRMINGHAM
B32 3NT

NASEN Enterprises Ltd.
2 Lichfield Road
STAFFORD
ST17 4JX

Thos. Nelson & Sons Ltd.
Nelson House
Mayfield Road
WALTON-ON-THAMES
Surrey
KT12 5PL

NES Arnold
Ludlow Hill Road
West Bridgford
NOTTINGHAM
NG2 6HD

N.F.E.R.- Nelson
Darville House
2 Oxford Road East
WINDSOR
Berkshire
SL4 1DF

Northern Micromedia Resources Centre
Coach Lane Campus
Coach Lane
NEWCASTLE UPON TYNE
NE7 7XA

Oliver & Boyd
FREEPOST
Pinnacles
HARLOW
Essex
CM19 4BR

Oxford University Press
Education Division
FREEPOST
Walton Street
OXFORD
OX2 6BR

Philip & Tacey Ltd.
North Way
ANDOVER
Hampshire
SP10 5BA

Scholastic Publications Ltd.
Westfield Road
Southam
LEAMINGTON SPA
Warwickshire
CV33 0JH

Sherston Software
Swan Barton
Sherston
MALMESBURY
Wilts.
SN16 0LH

Simon & Schuster Education
Campus 400
Maylands Avenue
HEMEL HEMPSTEAD
Herts
HP2 7EZ

Special Educational Needs (Marketing)
9 The Close
Church Aston
NEWPORT
Salop
TF10 9JL

Strathclyde Regional Council
Renfrew Division Psychological Service
Carbrook Street
PAISLEY
Renfrewshire
PA1 2NW

S.R.A. Ltd.
Newtown Road
HENLEY-ON-THAMES
Oxon
RG9 1EW

West Sussex County Council
Educational Publications
Education Department
County Hall
CHICHESTER
West Sussex
PO19 1RF

Wooden letters and numbers
for multisensory work from:
Westcraft
L.M. West
12 Sandhill Lane
Leeds Road,
SELBY
Yorks.
YO8 0JP

Whurr Publishers Ltd.
19b Compton Terrace
LONDON
N1 2UN

Wiltshire County Council
Advisory Services
County Hall
Towbridge
Wilts.

Xavier Educational Software Ltd.
Dept. of Psychology
UCNW BANGOR
Gwynedd
LL57 2DG

APPENDIX 5 COURSES IN SpLD FOR TEACHERS

Several teacher training colleges are now running their own courses in SpLD. It may be worth checking if there is one in your own area.

Information on other course locations and content can be obtained from the following contact addresses:

The Dyslexia Institute
Headquarters
133 Gresham Road
STAINES
Middlesex
TW18 2AJ
(0784 63851)

or
74 Victoria Crescent Road
Dowanhill
GLASGOW
G12 9JN
(041 334 4549)

Scheme Manager (Teachers of SpLD)
R.S.A.
Examinations Board
(Teacher/Trainer Qualifications)
Westwood Way
COVENTRY
CV4 8HS
(0203 470033
Fax. 0203 468080)

Mrs E. Miles
University College of North Wales
BANGOR
Gwynedd
LL57 2DG
(0248 351151)

The Hornsby Dyslexia Centre
71 Wandsworth Common Westside
LONDON
SW18 2ED
(081 871 2691)

APPENDIX 6 BIBLIOGRAPHY

ACKERMAN,A.,(1974), "Dyslexia: The Importance of Motivation", Helen Arkell Dyslexia Centre, London.

ALSTON,J. & TAYLOR,J.,(1987), "Handwriting: Theory, Research and Practice", Croom Helm, London.

ARBOR,A.,(1975), "Number Tracking", Ann Arbor Publishers, Belford.

ARKELL,H.,(1977), "Dyslexia: Introduction - A Dyslexic's Eye View", Helen Arkell Dyslexia Centre, London.

BARR,J.E.(1985), "Understanding Children Spelling", Scottish Council for Research in Education, Lindsay & Co., Edinburgh.

BRADLEY, L.,(1980) "Assessing Reading Difficulties: A Diagnostic and Remedial Approach", Macmillan Education.

BRYANT,P., & BRADLEY,L.,(1987), "Children's Reading Problems", Blackwell, Oxford.

BULLOCK (The Bullock Report),(1975), "A Language for Life", Committee of Enquiry into Reading and the Use of English, H.M.S.O., D.E.S.

BURGE,V.,(1986), "Dyslexia: Basic Numeracy", Helen Arkell Dyslexia Centre, Surrey.

BUZAN,T.,(1984), "Use Your Head", BBC Publications, London.

BUZAN,T.,(1986), "Use Your Memory", BBC Publications, London.

BUZAN,T.,(1988), "Make The Most Of Your Mind", Pan Books Ltd., London.

CHASTY,H & FRIEL,J.,(1991), "Children with Special Needs: Assessment, Law and Practice - Caught in the Act", Jessica Kingsley Publishers, London.

CHASTY,H. & PHILLIPS,M.,(1981), "Structured Cursive Handwriting", Ann Arbor, Belford.

CRATTY,B.J.,(1986), "Developmental Sequences of Perceptual- Motor Tasks", Prentice-Hall.

DEVEREUX,K.,(1982), "Understanding Learning Difficulties", Open University Press, Milton Keynes.

DONALDSON,M.,(1978), "Children's Minds", Collins, Glasgow.

FARNHAM-DIGGORY,(1984), "Learning Disabilities", The Chaucer Press, Bungay, Suffolk.

FERNALD,G.M., (1943) "Remedial Techniques in Basic School Subjects", McGraw-Hill, New York.

FRITH,U., (1980), "Cognitive Processes in Spelling", Academic Press, London.

GILLINGHAM,A.M. & STILLMAN,B.U. (1956), "Remedial Training for Children with Specific Disability in Reading, Spelling and Penmanship", 5th ed., Sackelt & Wilhelms, New York.

HICKEY,K.,(1977), "Dyslexia: A Language Training Course for Teachers and Learners." Kathleen Hickey, London. (For details of updated edition, see Appendix 2)

HORNSBY,B.,(1984), "Overcoming Dyslexia", Macdonald Optima, London.

HORNSBY,B. & SHEAR,F.,(1982), "Alpha to Omega: The A-Z of Teaching Writing and Spelling",Heinemann, London.

HULME,C.,(1981), "Reading Retardation and Multisensory Learning", Routledge & Kegan Paul, London.

HUNTER-CARSCH, M., (Ed.)(1989), "The Art of Reading", Blackwell, Oxford.

JORDAN, D.R.,(1072), "Dyslexia in the Classroom", Charles E. Merrill Publishing Co., Columbus, Ohio.

KINGMAN (1988), (The Kingman Report), "The Report of the Committee of Enquiry into the Teaching of English Language", H.M.S.O., D.E.S.

LAWRENCE,D.,(1973), "Improved Reading through Counselling", Ward Lock.

MACKAY,D., THOMPSON,B., & SCHAUB,P.,(1978), "Breakthrough to Literacy", Longman Schools Council Publication, London.

McDONALD,J., & HARKER,M.,(1988), "Teacher Initiated Monitoring and Evaluation" (TIME), Strathclyde Regional Psychological Service, Renfrew Division.

MICHAEL,B., & MICHAEL,M.,(1987), "Foundations of Writing: Learning to Write. Teachers' Guide", Jordanhill College, Glasgow - produced on behalf of Consultative Committee on the Curriculum, Committee on Primary Education

MILES,E.,(1989), "The Bangor Dyslexia Teaching System", Whurr Publishers Ltd.

MILES,T.R.,(1983), "The Bangor Dyslexia Test" from "Dyslexia - The Pattern of Difficulties", Granada, Cambridge.

MILES,T.R.,(1983b), "Dyslexia - The Pattern of Difficulties", Granada, Suffolk.

MILES,T.R., & MILES,E.,(1983), "Help for Dyslexic Children", Methuen, London.

MILLAR, R. & KLEIN, C.,(1986), "Making sense of Spelling: A Guide to Teaching and Learning How to Spell ", D.C.L.D., London.

MONTESSORI,M.,(1915), "The Montessori Method", Heineman, London.

MOYLE,D.,(1978), "Teaching Reading", Collection of seminars compiled and edited by Donald Moyle, Holmes McDougall, Edinburgh.

NEALE, M., (1989), "Neale Analysis of Reading Ability - Revised British Edition", NFER-Nelson.

POLLOK,J., & WALLER,E.,(1978), "Dyslexia: The Problems of Sequencing and Orientation", Helen Arkell Dyslexia Centre, London.

PUMFREY,P.,(1985), "Reading; Tests and Assessment Techniques", Hodder & Stoughton.

PUMFREY,P.D. & ELLIOTT,C.D. (Eds.), (1990) "Children's Difficulties in Reading, Spelling and Writing", The Falmer Press.

REASON,R., & BOOTE,R., (1989), "Learning Difficulties in Reading and Writing: A Teachers' Manual", NFER Nelson, Windsor.

ROSWELL,F.G. & NATCHEZ,G.,(1989), "Reading Disability: A Human Approach to Evaluation and Treatment of Reading and Writing Difficulties", Basic Books, New York.

RUSSELL,J.P.,(1988), "Graded Activities for Children with Motor Difficulties", Cambridge University Press, Cambridge.

SAMUELS,S.J.,(1978) (Ed.) "What Research has to say about Reading Instruction", International Reading Association, Newark, Delaware.

SCOTTISH CONSULTATIVE COMMITTEE ON THE CURRICULUM, (1989), "Hand in Your Writing", S.C.C.C., Dundee.

SELMES,I.,(1987), Improving Study Skills", Hodder & Stoughton, London.

SINGLETON,C.(Ed.), (1991), "Computers and Literacy Skills", Better Books.

SLINGERLAND,B.H.,(1971), "A Multisensory Approach to Language Arts for Specific Language Disability Children - A Guide for Primary Teachers", Educators Publishing Service, Cambridge, Massachusetts.

SLINGERLAND.B.H.,(1976), "Basics in Scope and Sequence of A Multi-sensory Approach to Language Arts for Specific Language Disability Children: A Guide for Primary Teachers in the Second-Year Continuum", Educators Publishing Service, Cambridge Massachusetts.

SNOWLING,M.,(1985), "Children's Written Language Difficulties", NFER Nelson, Windsor.

SNOWLING,M.,(1987), "Dyslexia: A Cognitive Developmental Perspective", Blackwell, Oxford.

SNOWLING,M. & THOMSON,M.,(1991), "Dyslexia: Integrating Theory and Practice", Whurr Publishers Ltd.

STIRLING,E.G.,(1985), "Help for the Dyslexic Adolescent", Better Books & St. David's College.

TANSLEY,P., & PANKHURST,J.,(1982), "Children with Specific Learning Difficulties: A Critical Review of Research", NFER, Surrey.

TAYLOR,R.,(1981), Coordinator "Ways and Means: Children with Learning Difficulties", Somerset Education Authority, Globe Educational, Basingstoke.

THOMSON,M & WATKINS,B.,(1990), "Dyslexia: A Teaching Handbook", Whurr Publishers Ltd.

TYLER,S. & ELLIOTT,C.D.,(1988), "Cognitive Profiles of Groups of Poor Readers and Dyslexic Children on the British Ability Scales", British Journal of Psychology, 79, 493-508.

VERNON,M.D.,(1971), "Reading and its Difficulties", Cambridge University Press, Cambridge.

WARNOCK,M.,(1978), "Special Educational Needs: Report of the Committee of Enquiry into the Education of Handicapped Children and Young People", H.M.S.O., London.

WENDON,L.,(1985,1987), "Letterland Teaching Programmes 1 and 2", Letterland Ltd., Cambridge.

WEST SUSSEX COUNTY COUNCIL,(1975), "Assessment of Intelligence", produced by W. Sussex County Education Committee: Psychological Service.

WIDLAKE, P.,(1977), "Remedial Education Programmes and Progress: A Reader", National Association for Remedial Education, Longman, London.

YOUNG,P., & TYRE,C.(1983), "Dyslexia or Illiteracy? Realising the Right to Read", The Open University Press, Milton Keynes.

Index

5-14 programme 10

acetate 27
acknowledgements ii
addition 38-41;
addresses (courses) 65
addresses (materials) 62 to 64
affixes 26
allowances 49
Alpha to Omega 23, 24
alphabet 19, 45
Ames, Ted 11
Ann Arbor 38
Appendices 51 to 68
area learning support 9
areas affected by SpLD 3
assessment 3, 5, 9, 11
assessment materials 51 to 53
assessment of reading 11
Aston Index 11, 13
audiometrician 8
auditory sequencing 6, 43
auditory sequential memory 46
auditory skills 45
auditory 20

Bangor Dyslexia Test 11
BAS 17
"beat the teacher" 41
bibliography 66
Bradley, Lynette 29
Breakthrough to Literacy 26

calculator 42
Calibre 48
checklist 6
checklist-early stages 6
checklist-later stages 8
chronological age 13
class teacher 7, 9
Clay, Marie 11
clocks 43
code 35
common 4
comprehension 11, 14, 15
computer software 24, 57 to 59
concentration 7
concepts 7
confusion 6
content 18
contents page iii
continuous prose 34
cooperative teaching 7
copying 6
correcting spelling 30
courses for teachers 65
creative arts 44

Cripps, Charles 29
criterion-referenced assessment 16, 37
curriculum 21, 22
curriculum-supportive skills 45
cursive writing 31

dictation 31
dictionary 19, 30
digital times 43
directional confusion 37
directionality 7
discrepancy 5
dominoes 42
drafting 34
dyslexia 1

early primary 6
Education Act (1981) 10
educational psychologist 9, 10, 17, 37
encouragement 18
English Picture Vocabulary Test 12
epilogue 50
exam work 49
Exercise Your Spelling 28
eyesight 8

5-14 programme 10
family history 6, 7
final blends 25
folio work 49
foreign languages 49
foreshortening 6
free writing 12
fusion 6

games 42-43, 61
general learning difficulties 3
general practitioner 8
Gillham and Hesse Basic Number Screening Test 37
Graded Activities for Children with Motor Difficulties 43

handwriting 31
handwriting material 56
headteacher 7, 9
hearing 8
Hickey, Kathleen 23, 27, 35
homework 18, 19, 30
homonyms 29
Hornsby and Shear 23
hospital 8
Hunt and Stab 25, 26

Improving Study Skills 49
incidence 4
inconsistency 8
individual programmes 21
initial blends 25

intellect 5
intellectual capacity 8
intention 2
interpretation of results 13
introduction i
irregular words 30

Keyboard Technology 42
Kim's Game 46
kinaesthetic 20

L.D.A. 34
language materials 54 to 60
language of maths 38
language 6
laterality 7
Learning Materials Ltd. 35
learning support co-ordinator 5, 9
legalities 2
Letterland 23, 24
Logical Spelling 28
look-and-say 20, 22
Look, Cover, Write & Check 29-30

Macmillan Diagnostic Reading Pack 11
mathematics 37 to 43
mechanics of reading 8
memory skills 19
memory 7, 45-47
mental age 13-15
mental arithmetic 7
Miles, Professor 12
mispronunciation 8
misunderstanding 8
mnemonic strategies 46
mnemonics 23, 31
"Money Box" 42
months 46
motivation 42, 43, 47
motor control 43
multiplication 39
multiplication facts 41
multiplication tables 7, 37, 41
multisensory 19, 38

naming 6
National Curriculum 10
nature 3
Neale Analysis 11
New Macmillan Reading Analysis 11
norm referenced testing 7
number bonds 41
number practice 39-41

O'Grady 41
observations 6
one-to-one correspondence 40
oral responses 18
organisational skills 19
orthoptist 8
overlearning 22

paired reading 26
parents 5, 9, 17, 41
Pelmanism 46
pencil grips 34
phonemes 23
phonics 20, 22
photocopying 48
physical education 43-44
placement 32
planning 44
positioning 18
prefix 25, 26
procedure for handwriting a phoneme 33
progress 6
proportion 4
provision 2
Psychological Service 16
puzzling 7

ratio 1
reading age 13
reading material 54 to 55
reading 11
reading 22 to 27
Really Useful Picture Series 35
Reason and Boote 23
Record of Needs 2, 5, 10
redrafting 34
remembering 6, 8
Renfrew Division 16
results 13
reversals 6
root 25
root 26
route to assessment 7, 9
Russell, Jim 43

S.O.S. technique 26, 29
school medical practitioner 8
scribe 49
seating position 33
secondary stage 48 to 49
Selmes, Ian 49
sequence for spelling 28
sequences 8, 46
sequencing 7, 37, 39, 45
severe difficulty 7
severity 4
shared reading 26
signs 5
sound-letter links 25
spatial awareness 37
specific learning difficulties 1
specific needs 21
spell-checking facility 48
spelling age 13-15
spelling assessment 11
spelling dictionaries 57
spelling material 55 to 56
spelling 22, 28 to 31
Stanford Binet 17
statement 2, 5, 10

Stirling, Eileen 30
structure 20, 35
structured cumulative multisensory methods 20
structured multisensory methods 21
suffix 25, 26
syllabification 25, 26
syntax 8

tape recorder 18, 27, 41, 49
technical difficulties 49
tenseness 6
terminology 1
TIME 16, 37, 38
time 18, 42-43
timetable 19,43
topic work 44

tramline paper 33
transposals 6

Vernon Spelling 11
Vernon-Miller Graded Arithmetic-Mathematics Test 37
visual perception 37
visual 20
visualisation 46, 47
vocabulary 48

Wendon, Lyn 23, 24
Westcraft 40
WISC 17, 37
word attack skills 25
word processor 34, 48
working memory 45

NOTES

NOTES

NOTES

Printed by William Anderson & Sons Limited, 34 Loanbank Quadrant, Glasgow G51 3HZ